TV Favorites

More Than 150 Popular Quick 'n' Easy Recipes

By Art Ginsburg
Mr. Food

Ginsburg Enterprises Incorporated
1770 NW 64th Street, Suite 500
Fort Lauderdale, Florida 33309

Library of Congress Cataloging-in-Publication Data

Ginsburg, Art.

Mr. Food TV Favorites: more than 150 popular quick 'n' easy recipes / by Art Ginsburg.

ISBN 978-0-615-32237-7
1. Cookery. I. Title: Mr. Food TV Favorites. II. Title

Printed in the United States of America

First Edition

www.mrfood.com

Table of Contents

Introduction

Where does the time go?!

It's hard to believe that I've been sharing mouthwatering recipes, timesaving and money-saving tips and lots more with you on TV for more than 30 years! Do you know the best part of it all for me? Meeting so many of you as I travel around the country, as well as having the opportunity to read your letters and emails. I thank you for those...please keep them coming! I love that you've become part of my family!

Can you guess the question I'm asked most often? "What are your most requested recipes?" Well, if you've been wondering the same thing, you've come to the right place, 'cause I'm answering that in this book. That's right, I've finally assembled a collection of my fan-favorite TV recipes all in one place for you.

They're all here – everything from Fancy Fast Chicken and Stacked Taco Salad to Chocolate Chip Cheesecake and, of course, my most requested recipe of all, my original version of Death by Chocolate. I'm sure you know by now that every one of my TV recipes has been thoroughly tested, tasted and retested numerous times, so these are the most popular, fool-proof recipes that you and my other loyal viewers and readers have given two thumbs up.

Enjoy making memories of your own with these "TV Favorites" that are truly timeless. And thank you for welcoming me into your home all these years and allowing me to be a part of your life every day, including holidays and so many other special occasions.

I love giving you and your gang more reasons to say...
"OOH IT'S SO GOOD!!®"

Art Ginsburg
(or, as you know me, "Mr. Food")

Amazing Appetizers

Artichoke-Spinach Spread

Serves 6 to 8

1 (10-ounce) package frozen chopped spinach, thawed and squeezed dry

1 (8-ounce) package cream cheese, softened

3/4 cup grated Parmesan cheese

1/4 cup mayonnaise

1 teaspoon lemon juice

1/4 teaspoon ground red pepper

1/4 teaspoon garlic powder

1 (14-ounce) can artichoke hearts, drained and chopped

1 Preheat oven to 350°F. Coat a 1-quart casserole dish with nonstick cooking spray.

2 In a medium bowl, combine all ingredients except artichoke hearts; beat until well blended. Stir in artichoke hearts then spoon into casserole dish.

3 Bake 30 to 35 minutes, or until heated through and edges are golden. Serve immediately.

PREPARATION TIP: For smaller gatherings, divide the uncooked mixture into smaller casserole dishes, wrap well, and keep them on hand in the freezer. That way, you can always heat up a treat for last-minute guests.

HEALTHY HINT: Watching your waistline but still want to indulge? Use light mayo and cream cheese, and serve with veggie sticks or my light, homemade Garlic Pita Crisps (page 160) for a guilt-free party-starter!

Dill Crab Dip

Serves 10 to 12

2 (8-ounce) packages
cream cheese, softened

1/2 pound imitation
crabmeat, flaked

1 teaspoon lemon juice

1 tablespoon fresh
chopped dill

1 Preheat oven to 350°F. In a medium bowl, combine all ingredients; mix well.

2 Spoon mixture into a 9-inch pie plate and bake 25 to 30 minutes, or until hot and bubbly. Serve immediately.

TV Tidbit: This proved to be impossible to keep on hand during the taping of my first half-hour holiday special. The crew kept digging in for "just a taste," resulting in my test kitchen director, Patty, having to stand guard over the on-camera dish! Turn back a page to see how awesome this looks!

Tex-Mex Dip

Serves 20 to 25

2 (9-ounce) cans bean dip

3 ripe avocados, mashed
(about 1-1/2 cups)

1/2 cup mayonnaise

1 tablespoon lemon juice

1 (16-ounce) container
sour cream

1 (1.25-ounce) package
taco seasoning mix

1-1/2 cups (6 ounces)
shredded Cheddar cheese

4 scallions, finely chopped

1 medium tomato, diced

1 Spread bean dip on a large serving tray (about a 12-inch round).

2 In a large bowl, combine avocados, mayonnaise, and lemon juice; spread over bean dip.

3 In a separate bowl, combine sour cream and taco seasoning mix; spread over first two layers. Sprinkle with the cheese then the scallions then the tomato. Cover loosely and refrigerate overnight to "marry" the flavors.

VIEWER FEEDBACK: You seem to love every recipe I do that's layered, from my Death by Chocolate and Seven-Layer Cookies to layered salads and this dip. It's a crowd-pleaser, for sure, and if you want to add a seventh layer, just add some sliced ripe olives after the cheese. Put it out with tortilla chips at your next party and stand back!

5

Roasted Red Pepper Hummus

Serves 8 to 10

2 (15-ounce) cans garbanzo beans (chickpeas), rinsed and drained, with 1/3 cup liquid reserved

1 (12-ounce) jar roasted red peppers, drained

3 garlic cloves

2 tablespoons lemon juice

2 tablespoons olive oil

1 teaspoon ground cumin

1 teaspoon salt

1 In a food processor, combine all ingredients, including reserved garbanzo bean liquid. Process until mixture is smooth and no lumps remain, scraping down sides of bowl as needed.

2 Serve immediately, or cover and chill until ready to use.

HEALTHY HINT: Beans are a great source of fiber, so this rich and creamy spread is a staple in healthy meal plans. And you can make it any flavor you want: Leave out the roasted peppers and enjoy it plain or add your favorite ingredients like chopped ripe olives, pesto sauce or almost anything else to the plain version. Any flavor will be a winner!

Pizza Fondue

Serves 6 to 8

1/2 pound ground beef

2 cups spaghetti sauce

1-1/2 cups (6 ounces) shredded mozzarella cheese

1/4 cup grated Parmesan cheese

1/2 teaspoon dried oregano

1 loaf Italian bread, cut into 1-inch cubes

1 In a medium skillet, brown the ground beef over medium-high heat for 4 to 6 minutes, until crumbled and no pink remains.

2 In a medium saucepan, combine spaghetti sauce, mozzarella and Parmesan cheeses, and oregano over medium-high heat, stirring until cheeses are melted.

3 Add crumbled ground beef and cook until heated through. Pour into a fondue pot and serve with bread cubes for dipping.

DID YOU KNOW... I call fondue "The Comeback Kid"? It was popular for house parties back in the '70s and it's had a real resurgence lately, probably because Boomers remembered what an easy, tasty and fun party food it is!

Sweet-and-Sour Meatballs

Makes about 32 cocktail-sized meatballs

2 pounds ground beef

1 egg

1/4 cup dry bread crumbs

1 teaspoon salt

1/2 teaspoon onion powder

1/8 teaspoon black pepper

1 (12-ounce) jar
    cocktail sauce

1/2 cup grape jelly

3 tablespoons lemon juice

1 In a large bowl, combine ground beef, egg, bread crumbs, salt, onion powder, and pepper; mix well. Form into 1-inch meatballs and set aside.

2 In a medium saucepan, combine cocktail sauce, jelly, and lemon juice. Bring to a boil over medium-high heat.

3 Add uncooked meatballs to saucepan, reduce heat to low, cover, and simmer 15 minutes, without stirring (so meatballs will set).

4 Stir gently then simmer 25 more minutes, stirring occasionally. Remove from heat when meatballs are cooked through.

SERVING TIP: These are really best when they're prepared a day before serving. Cover and refrigerate overnight then skim fat off top and heat to serve.

Marinated Steak Nachos

Serves 10 to 12

1/2 cup lemon juice

2 tablespoons minced garlic

1 tablespoon dried oregano

1 tablespoon ground cumin

1 teaspoon salt

1 tablespoon black pepper

1 (1-1/2-pound) beef flank steak

1 (14-ounce) package tortilla chips

2 cups (8 ounces) shredded Colby Jack cheese blend

2 large tomatoes, seeded and chopped

3 scallions, thinly sliced

1 In a large resealable plastic storage bag, combine lemon juice, garlic, oregano, cumin, salt, and pepper. Add flank steak, seal, and shake gently to completely coat steak. Marinate in refrigerator 30 minutes.

2 Preheat broiler. Place steak on a rimmed baking sheet; discard marinade. Broil 8 to 9 minutes per side for medium, or until desired doneness beyond that.

3 Allow to cool 10 minutes. Place on a cutting board and cut across grain into thin slices then cut into 1-inch pieces. Spread tortilla chips over two large rimmed baking sheets or oven-proof platters then top evenly with sliced steak and sprinkle with cheese. Reduce oven temperature to 350°F. and bake 5 to 6 minutes, or until cheese has melted.

4 Remove nachos from oven; sprinkle with tomatoes and scallions. Serve immediately.

SERVING TIP: Get into the party spirit by serving these with chopped green chilies, jalapeño peppers, olives, salsa, sour cream, or other favorite toppings. And for adults only, serve up some icy cold Margaritas in salt-rimmed glasses to create a Mexican fiesta in your own home!

Bacon-Wrapped Scallops

Makes about 2 dozen

3/4 pound bacon

1 pound sea scallops, rinsed and patted dry (see note)

1 cup ketchup

1/3 cup packed light brown sugar

1/2 cup white vinegar

1 Preheat oven to 425°F.

2 Cut bacon slices in half crosswise. Roll a piece of bacon around each scallop and secure with a wooden toothpick; place on rimmed baking sheet.

3 Bake 15 to 18 minutes, or until scallops are cooked through and bacon is crisp.

4 Meanwhile, in a medium saucepan, combine ketchup, brown sugar, and vinegar over medium heat; mix well and cook 5 to 7 minutes, until sugar is dissolved.

5 Dip bacon-wrapped scallops in sauce and serve with remaining sauce.

VIEWER FEEDBACK: The most frequent question I get about seafood is how to tell the difference between sea scallops and bay scallops. Sea scallops, more common and widely available, are large (20 to 30 per pound), while bay scallops, used in casseroles, stews and stir-fry dishes, are small (up to 90 per pound). Remember it this way: The sea is larger than the bay! Good trick, huh?

Pistachio-Stuffed Mushrooms

Makes 16 mushrooms

16 large mushrooms
(about 1 pound total)

6 tablespoons
(3/4 stick) butter

1/2 small onion,
minced

1/4 cup pistachios,
finely chopped

1/3 cup plain
bread crumbs

2 tablespoons
chopped fresh
parsley

1/4 teaspoon salt

1/4 teaspoon
black pepper

1 Preheat oven to 350°F.

2 Remove mushroom stems from caps; set aside caps and finely chop stems.

3 In a large skillet, melt butter over medium heat. Add chopped mushroom stems, onion, and pistachios, and sauté until vegetables are tender.

4 Remove from heat and stir in remaining ingredients except mushroom caps; mix well then stuff each mushroom cap equally with pistachio mixture and place on a large rimmed baking sheet.

5 Bake 20 to 25 minutes, or until mushrooms are tender.

TV Tidbit: Several years ago, I had a blast shooting segments in the California pistachio fields. Getting an up-close look at how they grow allowed me to share firsthand information on my shows. And I've gotta admit that I really enjoyed nibbling on handful after handful of pistachios between takes! You could say I'm "nuts" about pistachios!

Crispy Coconut Shrimp

Serves 4 to 6

1/2 cup all-purpose flour

1 tablespoon sugar

1 teaspoon ground red pepper

1/2 teaspoon salt

2 eggs

2 tablespoons water

2-1/2 cups sweetened
flaked coconut

1 pound large shrimp, peeled
and deveined, with tails
left on

2 cups vegetable oil

1 In a shallow dish, combine flour, sugar, ground red pepper, and salt; mix well.

2 In a medium bowl, beat together the eggs and water. Place coconut in another shallow dish. Coat shrimp in flour mixture then dip in egg mixture. Roll in coconut, pressing it firmly onto both sides of the shrimp to coat completely.

3 In a large saucepan, heat oil over medium heat. Cook shrimp, in batches, for 1-1/2 to 2 minutes, or until golden, turning once during cooking. Drain on a paper towel-lined platter, and serve.

SERVING TIP: Try these with a sweet-and-sour dipping sauce; they make wonderful appetizers. Or serve 'em with wild rice for a scrumptious company-fancy main dish.

Thai Chicken Satay

Serves 12

24 wooden skewers

1 pound boneless, skinless chicken breast, cut into 24 strips

1/2 cup reduced-fat or regular creamy peanut butter

2 tablespoons light soy sauce

2 teaspoons sesame oil

1 tablespoon butter

2 teaspoons crushed red pepper

1 Soak wooden skewers in water 15 to 20 minutes. Preheat oven to 350°F.

2 Thread chicken onto skewers and place on a rimmed baking sheet.

3 In a small saucepan, combine remaining ingredients over low heat until melted and smooth. Brush evenly over chicken skewers, completely coating chicken.

4 Bake 8 to 10 minutes, or until chicken is cooked through and no pink remains.

DID YOU KNOW...
the dish known as "satay" originated in Indonesia? It was first sold by street vendors before eventually becoming popular all over Southeast Asia. Here in the West, satay is a mainstay on Thai restaurant menus.

Pepperoni Pie Squares

Serves 8 to 10

1-1/2 cups all-purpose flour

2 cups milk

2 eggs, lightly beaten

1 pound Muenster cheese, cubed

1 (8-ounce) package sliced pepperoni, chopped

1 teaspoon dried Italian seasoning

1 Preheat oven to 350°F. Coat a 9" x 13" baking dish with nonstick cooking spray.

2 In a large bowl, combine all ingredients; mix well then pour into baking dish.

3 Bake 25 to 30 minutes, until top is golden; cool slightly then cut into squares. Serve as is or topped with warm marinara or pizza sauce.

TV Tidbit: This recipe is a classic from one of my earliest shows, and every few years I share it again for my next generation of viewers. It's so good, I usually make an extra batch for the newsroom, where they nibble on it during commercial breaks!

Game-Day Wings

Makes 50 to 55 split wings

1/4 cup packed brown sugar

1 tablespoon ground ginger

2 teaspoons garlic powder

1/4 teaspoon crushed
red pepper

1/2 cup dry white wine

1 (10-ounce) bottle soy sauce

5 pounds split chicken wings
or drumettes, thawed if
frozen (see Option)

1 Preheat oven to 350°F. Coat 2 rimmed baking sheets with nonstick cooking spray.

2 In a large bowl, combine all ingredients except chicken wings; mix well. Add chicken and toss to coat. Cover and chill 2 hours (see Option).

3 Drain wings well and place on baking sheets; discard remaining marinade.

4 Bake wings 30 minutes then turn them over. Baste wings with pan juices then bake 30 more minutes, until cooked through and golden.

OPTION: If you want to start with whole wings and split them yourself before cooking, split them at each joint and discard the tips. This makes them much easier to eat. Also, these can marinate for up to 2 days in the fridge.

VIEWER FEEDBACK: My test kitchen team came up with these babies during football season a while back. I knew when I tasted them that they were gonna score big points with my viewers! Try 'em yourself and taste why!

Super Soups & Salads

Mexican Tortilla Soup

Serves 6 to 8

1 tablespoon vegetable oil

1 pound boneless, skinless chicken breasts, cut into 1/2-inch chunks

1 red bell pepper, coarsely chopped

3 garlic cloves, minced

3 (14-ounce) cans ready-to-serve reduced-sodium chicken broth

1 (10-ounce) package frozen whole kernel corn

1/2 cup salsa

1/4 cup chopped fresh cilantro

1 cup broken-up baked tortilla chips

1 In a soup pot, heat oil over medium heat. Add chicken, bell pepper, and garlic, and cook about 3 minutes, or until chicken is browned, stirring frequently.

2 Stir in chicken broth, corn, and salsa; bring to a boil. Reduce heat to low, cover, and simmer 5 minutes, or until no pink remains in chicken.

3 Stir in cilantro, ladle soup into bowls, and serve topped with tortilla chips.

MAKE IT A COMPLETE MEAL: Serve **Pepper-Jack Quesadillas** with this flavor-packed soup. For each quesadilla, simply sprinkle 1/2 cup shredded Monterey Jack-pepper cheese over a 10-inch tortilla and top with another tortilla. Cook the "tortilla sandwich" in a large nonstick skillet in 1/2 teaspoon vegetable oil for 3 to 4 minutes, or until the cheese is melted, turning halfway through cooking. Cut into wedges and serve with your favorite toppers.

Italian Wedding Soup

Serves 8 to 10

6 (10-1/2-ounce) cans *condensed* chicken broth

6 cups water

Mini meatballs (see below)

4 cups fresh chopped escarole

3/4 cup grated Parmesan cheese, plus extra for garnish

2 eggs, beaten

1 In a large soup pot, bring chicken broth and water to a boil over high heat. Carefully add meatballs to broth and cook 5 to 7 minutes, or until no pink remains (see below).

2 Reduce heat to medium-low, add escarole, and cook 4 to 5 minutes, or until tender. Stir in 3/4 cup cheese then gradually stir in beaten eggs, forming strands. Serve immediately as is or topped with a sprinkle of Parmesan cheese.

Mini Meatballs

Makes about 6 dozen

1/2 pound lean ground beef

1/2 pound hot Italian sausage, casings removed

1 egg

1 small onion, minced

1/2 cup Italian-seasoned bread crumbs

1 teaspoon garlic powder

1/2 teaspoon salt

1/4 teaspoon black pepper

1 In a large bowl, combine all ingredients; mix well. Using a 1/2-teaspoon measure, shape into 1-inch meatballs.

2 Add meatballs to soup and cook as directed above, or sauté meatballs in a skillet for 5 to 10 minutes, until browned, before adding to soup.

DID YOU KNOW...this soup never had anything to do with a wedding? In Italian, the words *minestra maritata* literally translate to "married soup" and the story is that it got its name from the "marriage" of the vegetables and the meat! Whether or not that's true, it's a great story!

French Onion Soup

Serves 4 to 6

3 tablespoons butter

3 large onions, thinly sliced

3 (14-ounce) cans
ready-to-serve beef broth

1 cup apple cider

1/2 teaspoon black pepper

1/2 cup grated Parmesan
cheese

1/3 cup dry red wine

4 to 6 (1-inch) slices
French bread, toasted

1/2 cup shredded Swiss
cheese

1 In a soup pot, melt butter over medium heat. Add onions and cook 25 minutes, or until golden, stirring occasionally.

2 Add beef broth, apple cider, and black pepper; bring to a boil. Reduce heat to low, stir in Parmesan cheese and wine, and cook 3 to 5 minutes, or until cheese is melted and soup is heated through.

3 Preheat broiler. Place bread on a baking sheet and sprinkle with equal amounts of Swiss cheese. Broil 3 to 5 minutes, or until cheese is melted.

4 Pour soup into bowls and top each with a slice of toasted cheese bread; serve.

TV Tidbit: I have to give credit where credit is due, and this recipe came from my executive producer, who happens to be an incredible cook. I think you'll agree that the secret ingredient here, apple cider, makes this soup a show-stopper!

Hearty Minestrone

Serves 10 to 12

3 (14-ounce) cans ready-to-serve beef broth

1 (15-ounce) can red kidney beans, undrained

1 (20-ounce) can cannellini beans, undrained

1 (28-ounce) can crushed tomatoes

1 (10-ounce) package frozen chopped spinach, thawed

1 (10-ounce) package frozen mixed vegetables, thawed

1 small onion, chopped

1 teaspoon garlic powder

1 teaspoon salt

1/2 teaspoon black pepper

1 cup uncooked elbow macaroni

1 In a soup pot, combine all ingredients except the macaroni. Bring to a boil over medium-high heat.

2 Stir in macaroni, reduce heat to low and simmer 30 minutes, until macaroni is tender, stirring occasionally.

HEALTHY HINT: The more veggies, the better! I like to add chopped red cabbage to this when I have it, since it's yummy and packed with antioxidants.

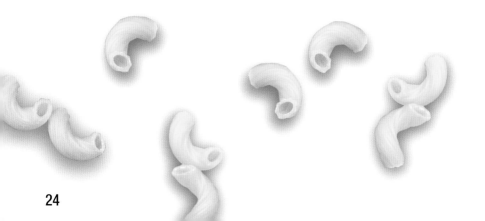

Steakhouse Soup

Serves 6 to 8

2 tablespoons vegetable oil

1-1/2 pounds (1/2-inch-thick) boneless beef top sirloin steak, trimmed and cut into thin strips (see Tip)

1/2 pound fresh mushrooms, sliced

1 large sweet onion, chopped

3 (14-ounce) cans ready-to-serve beef broth

4 cups water

1/2 cup dry red wine

3 large potatoes, scrubbed and cut into 1/2-inch cubes

2 teaspoons steak seasoning

2 cups (8 ounces) shredded Monterey Jack cheese

1 In a soup pot, heat oil over medium-high heat. Add steak strips, mushrooms, and onion, and cook 12 to 15 minutes, or until steak is browned and onion is tender.

2 Add remaining ingredients except cheese and bring to a boil. Reduce heat to low, cover, and simmer 25 to 30 minutes, or until steak and potatoes are tender. Ladle into bowls and serve sprinkled with shredded cheese.

TIMESAVING TIP: Supermarket butchers are usually happy to trim and cut beef the way we need it. Ask to have it cut this way, and save yourself some prep time.

Broccoli Cheese Soup

Serves 8 to 10

- 3 (14-ounce) cans ready-to-serve chicken broth
- 1 head broccoli, trimmed and chopped
- 1 small onion, diced
- 1 teaspoon black pepper
- 1/2 cup (1 stick) butter
- 1/2 cup all-purpose flour
- 1 cup (1/2 pint) heavy cream
- 3 cups (12 ounces) shredded Cheddar cheese

1 In a soup pot, combine broth, broccoli, onion, and pepper; bring to a boil over high heat then reduce heat to low, cover, and simmer 25 to 30 minutes, or until broccoli is very tender.

2 Meanwhile, in a medium skillet, melt butter over medium heat. Add flour and stir until well combined and browned.

3 Gradually stir butter mixture into soup, until soup is thickened. Gradually add heavy cream, mixing constantly.

4 Add cheese 1 cup at a time, mixing well after each addition, until melted.

TIMESAVING TIP:
Take advantage of the supermarket shortcut of bagged pre-cut broccoli. Just remember to wash it well before using, as you should all your produce.

Icy Hot Gazpacho

Serves 10

1 (14-1/2-ounce) can diced tomatoes, drained

1 (46-ounce) can no-salt-added tomato juice

1 large cucumber, peeled, seeded, and diced

1 medium-sized green bell pepper, diced

5 scallions, thinly sliced

3 garlic cloves, minced

1/3 cup white vinegar

1 tablespoon olive oil

2 tablespoons Worcestershire sauce

1/2 teaspoon hot pepper sauce

1 In a large bowl, combine all ingredients; mix well.

2 Cover and chill at least 4 hours before serving.

HEALTHY HINT: This is a nutritious make-ahead favorite you can keep in the fridge for when everybody comes home hungry. To give it a little extra flair, top each serving with a swirl of low-fat sour cream and a sprig of fresh dill.

Saucy White Chili

Serves 8 to 10

1 tablespoon vegetable oil

6 skinless, boneless chicken breast halves (1-1/2 to 2 pounds total), cut into 1-inch cubes

1/4 teaspoon salt

1/4 teaspoon black pepper

1 medium-sized onion, chopped

1 teaspoon minced garlic

5 (16-ounce) cans Great Northern beans, undrained

1 (14-1/2-ounce) can whole tomatoes, undrained, broken up

1 (4-ounce) can chopped green chilies, undrained

2 (14-ounce) cans ready-to-serve chicken broth

2 teaspoons ground cumin

1 teaspoon chili powder

1 In a soup pot, heat oil over medium heat. Sprinkle chicken with salt and pepper, and sauté 5 to 6 minutes, until browned.

2 Add onion and garlic, and cook 3 to 4 minutes, or until onion is tender. Add remaining ingredients and bring to a boil.

3 Reduce heat to low and simmer 50 to 60 minutes, or until chili thickens slightly, stirring ocasionally.

SERVING TIP: If you want to make this even heartier, spoon it over hot cooked rice, and put out serving bowls of chopped tomatoes, cheese and your other favorite chili toppers.

Tomato Bread Salad

Serves 4 to 6

4 ripe tomatoes, seeded and cut into 1-inch chunks

1/2 cup Italian dressing

3-1/2 cups toasted bread cubes or packaged croutons (see Tip)

1 medium cucumber, seeded and cubed

1/2 large red onion, thinly sliced

2 teaspoons Italian seasoning

1/4 teaspoon black pepper

1 (8-ounce) package mixed greens, optional

1 In a large bowl, combine tomatoes and dressing; mix well and marinate at least 15 minutes.

2 Stir in remaining ingredients except mixed greens; toss and serve as is or over mixed greens.

PREPARATION TIP: Making your own toasted bread cubes is a snap! Place bread cubes in a single layer in a baking dish and bake in a preheated 375°F. oven 15 minutes, or until golden, stirring twice. Allow to cool before using in this or any other salad.

TV Tidbit: My wife Ethel, a.k.a. "Mrs. Food," is always at my tapings to handle my wardrobe. When I started this show, as I cut the tomato, it squirted all over me. What a mess! Ethel rushed in with a clean apron, and I started again. You can bet I was extra careful with "take two!" *(Thanks, Ethel, for always being there to help me look my best on & off camera!)*

Asian Cabbage Salad

Makes 2 cups

2 tablespoons peanut oil

1/2 cup sesame seeds

4 cloves garlic, minced

2 tablespoons soy sauce

1/4 cup white vinegar

1/2 cup sugar

3/4 cup vegetable oil

1 head Napa or Chinese cabbage, washed and cut into bite-sized pieces

1 In a medium saucepan, warm peanut oil over medium heat. Sauté sesame seeds and garlic 3 to 5 minutes, until seeds are golden.

2 Reduce heat to medium-low and add soy sauce, vinegar, sugar and vegetable oil; continue to cook 2 more minutes.

3 Place cabbage in a large bowl and pour desired amount of warm dressing over it, tossing to coat cabbage evenly. (If you have extra dressing, it will hold in the refrigerator for up to 1 month. Just reheat before adding to more cabbage.)

SERVING TIP: Sprinkle store-bought Chinese noodles over this for extra crunch, and pass out the chopsticks. It's fun to eat with chopsticks when you know what you're doing, and even more fun to watch someone else who doesn't!

Stacked Taco Salad

Serves 8 to 10

- 1 pound ground beef
- 1 (1-1/4-ounce) package dry taco seasoning mix
- 1 medium head iceberg lettuce, chopped
- 2 cups (8 ounces) shredded Cheddar cheese
- 1 (6-ounce) can dark red kidney beans, rinsed and drained
- 2 large tomatoes, diced
- 2 (2-1/4-ounce) cans sliced black olives, drained
- 1 (14-1/2-ounce) bag ranch-flavored tortilla chips, crushed
- 1 (16-ounce) bottle sweet-and-spicy French salad dressing

1 In a medium skillet, brown ground beef with taco seasoning mix over medium-high heat, stirring to break up meat; drain and cool.

2 In an extra-large salad bowl, layer half the lettuce then half the cheese, beans, ground beef, tomatoes, and olives. Repeat layers then top with crushed tortilla chips. Bring salad to table and, just before serving, add dressing and toss until ingredients are well coated.

VIEWER FEEDBACK: After this show aired, I enjoyed hearing from a viewer who said her son and his friends ate the entire bag of tortilla chips she was going to use to make this! The viewer found a box of taco shells in her pantry, crushed them up and sprinkled them on the salad. Her quick thinking saved the day…and her salad!

Sunshine Salad

Serves 6

3/4 pound mixed baby greens

1 pint fresh strawberries, washed, hulled, and sliced

2 oranges, peeled and sliced

1 (8-ounce) bottle Italian dressing

1/2 small onion, finely chopped

1/3 cup granulated sugar

1/2 cup crumbled blue cheese

1 In a large salad bowl, combine baby greens, strawberries, and oranges.

2 In a small bowl, combine remaining ingredients except blue cheese; mix well and add to greens and fruit mixture. Toss, sprinkle with blue cheese, and serve.

SERVING TIP: If you want to make this in advance, chill the salad then toss with the dressing mixture and add blue cheese just before serving.

Mexican Corn Bread Salad

Serves 8 to 10

1 (1-ounce) package dry ranch-style dressing mix

1 cup sour cream

1 cup mayonnaise

6 corn bread muffins (16 ounces total)

2 (16-ounce) cans pinto beans, rinsed and drained

1 medium-sized green bell pepper, chopped

2 (15-1/4-ounce) cans whole-kernel corn, drained

3 large tomatoes, chopped

10 slices bacon, cooked and crumbled

2 cups (8 ounces) shredded Mexican cheese blend

6 scallions, sliced

1 In a small bowl, combine dressing mix, sour cream, and mayonnaise; set aside.

2 Crumble half of the corn muffins into a large glass bowl or trifle dish. In this order, add layers of half of the: beans, bell pepper, sour cream mixture, corn, tomatoes, bacon, cheese, and scallions. Repeat layers with the remaining half of each ingredient.

3 Cover and chill at least 2 hours before serving.

HEALTHY OPTIONS: Hey, all you waistline-watchers, don't skip this one! Simply use light versions of the sour cream, mayo, and shredded cheese. And that bacon can be turkey bacon. With a recipe this good, you'll still be able to indulge!

Grilled Romaine

Serves 6

3 tablespoons olive oil

2 garlic cloves, minced

1 tablespoon lemon juice

1/2 teaspoon salt

3 fresh whole romaine hearts, cut in half lengthwise *with core intact*

Fresh ground pepper

1 Preheat grill to medium heat.

2 In a small bowl, combine olive oil, garlic, lemon juice, and salt. Brush mixture on cut sides of romaine and season with fresh ground pepper.

3 Grill cut-side down for 5 minutes, or until lettuce just starts to brown. Turn and cook until wilted and golden. Serve warm.

SERVING TIP: What better to drizzle over warm grilled lettuce than homemade Warm Bacon Dressing? I think you'll get raves if you try mine – it's a gift I couldn't resist giving you!

Warm Bacon Dressing

Makes about 1-3/4 cups

1 pound bacon, diced

1/2 cup apple cider vinegar

1 tablespoon lemon juice

1/4 cup sugar

1/2 teaspoon black pepper

1 In a large skillet, cook bacon over medium-high heat until crisp.

2 Add remaining ingredients; mix well, and serve warm. Refrigerate any left-over dressing and reheat before serving.

Garbage Salad

Serves 10 to 12

1 head iceberg lettuce

1 head romaine lettuce

2 medium tomatoes

6 (1-ounce) slices provolone cheese, cut into strips

6 ounces Genoa salami, cut into strips

1 (14-ounce) can hearts of palm, drained and cut

1 (14-ounce) can artichoke hearts, drained and quartered

1 (7-ounce) jar roasted red peppers, drained and cut into strips

1 (5.75-ounce) can large pitted black olives, drained

1 (16-ounce) jar peperoncini, drained

Prepared vinaigrette dressing (about 2-1/4 cups)

1 Wash and dry lettuce and tomatoes then cut into bite-sized pieces. Place in an extra-large mixing bowl with remaining ingredients except dressing; toss to mix well.

2 Pour desired amount of dressing over salad; toss to coat. Serve immediately.

TV Tidbit: My show is seen on local news stations around the U.S. and I've been on TV for so long in Chicago, it's like my hometown! When we shot outside Gibson's, a landmark Chicago steakhouse, so many folks honked their car horns and shouted "OOH IT'S SO GOOD!!" that we gave up and moved the cameras inside! Enjoy this phenomenal salad modeled after the signature Gibson's dish.

Pleasing Poultry

Apricot-Glazed Cornish Hens

Serves 4 to 8

1 medium orange, quartered

4 Cornish hens

1/2 teaspoon salt

1/4 teaspoon black pepper

1 cup apricot preserves

1/2 cup packed light brown sugar

1 Preheat oven to 350°F. Coat a roasting pan with nonstick cooking spray.

2 Place an orange quarter into the cavity of each Cornish hen and place them in pan. Season with salt and pepper.

3 In a small bowl, combine preserves and brown sugar, and pour mixture over hens. Roast, uncovered, for 1-1/4 to 1-1/2 hours, or until no pink remains and juices run clear, basting every 20 minutes. Serve whole or cut each hen in half, and serve with additional glaze from pan spooned over the top.

HEALTHY OPTIONS: Sprinkle with a few sliced toasted almonds and serve with my awesome Glazed Baby Carrots.

Glazed Baby Carrots

Serves 4 to 6

2 tablespoons white vinegar

1/4 teaspoon cornstarch

1/2 cup packed light brown sugar

2 tablespoons butter

1 (16-ounce) package fresh whole baby carrots, blanched *or* frozen carrots, thawed

1 In a medium saucepan, combine vinegar and cornstarch; mix until cornstarch is dissolved. Add brown sugar and butter.

2 Bring mixture to a boil over medium heat, stirring until thickened. Add carrots, and cook 3 to 5 minutes, or until heated through. Serve immediately.

Chicken & Broccoli Turnovers

Serves 8

1 (10-3/4-ounce) can condensed broccoli cheese soup, divided

1/2 cup milk

1 (10-ounce) package refrigerated cooked and sliced chicken breast, coarsely chopped

1 (10-ounce) package frozen chopped broccoli, thawed and drained

1/4 teaspoon black pepper

1 (17.3-ounce) package frozen puff pastry, thawed

1 Preheat oven to 375°F. In a medium saucepan, combine 1/2 cup soup and the milk; set aside.

2 In a medium bowl, combine remaining soup, the chicken, broccoli, and pepper; mix well.

3 With a rolling pin, roll out each puff pastry sheet to a 12-inch square. Cut each sheet into 4 equal squares. Place an equal amount of chicken mixture in center of each square. Fold pastry over filling, forming triangles. With your finger or a fork, pinch or press edges together firmly to seal.

4 Place turnovers on 2 large rimmed baking sheets. Bake 20 to 22 minutes, or until golden. Heat soup and milk mixture over medium heat until hot and bubbly, stirring occasionally. Spoon over turnovers and serve.

VIEWER FEEDBACK: I really enjoy reading comments viewers send me about my recipes, like the one I got from a grateful mom after this recipe aired: "Mr. Food, I finally got my finicky son to eat broccoli – your recipe did the trick! A million thanks to you!"

Fancy Fast Chicken

Serves 6

6 bone-in chicken breast halves, skinned (see Note)

6 (1-ounce) slices Swiss cheese

1/4 pound fresh mushrooms, sliced (optional)

1 (10-3/4-ounce) can *condensed* cream of chicken soup

1/2 cup dry white wine

2 cups dry herb-seasoned stuffing mix

1 stick butter, melted

1 Preheat oven to 350°F. Lightly grease a 9″ x 13″ baking pan.

2 Place chicken in pan and top each piece with a slice of Swiss cheese. Arrange sliced mushrooms over cheese, if desired.

3 In a small bowl, combine soup and wine; pour over chicken. Sprinkle with stuffing mix then drizzle with melted butter.

4 Bake 50 to 60 minutes, or until chicken is done.

NOTE: If you'd rather use boneless and skinless chicken breast halves, only bake this 45 to 50 minutes, or until cooked through.

TV Tidbit: This one goes back to my earliest days on television and, let me tell you, it was one of the biggest hits I've had! As a matter of fact, it's still my most requested chicken recipe after more than 30 years of shows! It *must* be good!

Quick-as-a-Wink Pesto Chicken

Serves 4

4 (4-ounce) boneless, skinless chicken breast cutlets

4 tablespoons prepared pesto sauce

4 slices (3 ounces total) mozzarella cheese

1 Coat a large skillet with nonstick cooking spray and heat over medium-high heat.

2 Cook chicken 3 to 4 minutes per side, or until browned.

3 Top each chicken breast with 1 tablespoon pesto sauce and 1 slice of mozzarella cheese. Cover, and cook 2 to 3 minutes, or until no pink remains in chicken. Serve immediately.

SERVING TIP: A simple way to fancy this up is to top each serving with thin slices of plum tomato and a sprig of fresh basil. I keep pots of herbs on my windowsill and snip pieces as I need 'em. Do you keep fresh herbs handy, too? It sure is a great way to add natural, fresh flavor to loads of foods!

Chicken Strudel

Serves 4 to 6

1 cup cooked chicken chunks (each about 1/2″)

1 (10-ounce) package frozen chopped asparagus, thawed and drained

1 (17-ounce) jar Alfredo sauce, divided

1 sheet (from 17.3-ounce package) frozen puff pastry, thawed

Nonstick cooking spray

1 Preheat oven to 400°F. In a medium bowl, combine chicken, asparagus, and 3/4 cup Alfredo sauce; mix well.

2 Unfold puff pastry onto a large baking sheet. Spoon chicken mixture lengthwise down center of pastry. Cut slits 1 inch apart lengthwise down each side of filling.

3 Braid dough over filling, overlapping to form "X" shapes. Spray top with nonstick cooking spray.

4 Bake 25 to 27 minutes, or until heated through and golden.

5 In a small saucepan, heat remaining Alfredo sauce over low heat. Slice strudel and serve topped with sauce.

OPTIONS: Instead of chicken, try cooked turkey, or leftover cooked meat or fish. This also makes a hit as an appetizer.

Honey Chicken

Serves 4 to 6

1 cup all-purpose flour

1-1/2 teaspoons baking powder

1/2 teaspoon salt

3/4 cup water

1/3 cup sesame seeds

Vegetable oil for frying

1-1/2 pounds boneless, skinless chicken breasts, cut into 1-inch chunks

1/2 cup honey

2 garlic cloves, minced

1/4 teaspoon soy sauce

1 In a large bowl, make a batter by combining flour, baking powder, salt, and water; mix well.

2 In a large deep skillet, toast sesame seeds over medium-high heat, until golden. Remove from skillet and set aside.

3 Reduce heat to medium, add 1/4 inch oil to skillet, and heat oil until hot but not smoking. Dip chicken pieces in batter, coating completely, then cook in batches 2 to 3 minutes per side, or until golden. Drain on a paper towel-lined platter.

4 Meanwhile, in a medium saucepan, warm honey, garlic, and soy sauce over low heat 4 to 6 minutes, stirring occasionally. Place chicken in a large bowl and pour warm honey sauce over it. Sprinkle with sesame seeds, and toss until chicken is well coated. Serve immediately.

TV Tidbit: Every time I make a recipe with honey, I think back to the time I shot shows at a bee farm and wore a bee suit (no, not a bumblebee costume, but a protective suit worn by professional beekeepers) while discussing honey's health benefits. I looked pretty goofy, especially in the enormous helmet, but at least I didn't get stung!

Garlic Lover's Chicken

Serves 4

1 (3- to 3-1/2-pound) whole chicken

1/4 cup olive oil

1 tablespoon finely chopped fresh basil

1 teaspoon salt

1/2 teaspoon black pepper

1 head garlic, separated into cloves (about 15)

1 Preheat oven to 350°F. Place chicken in a roasting pan; set aside.

2 In a small bowl, mix together oil, basil, salt, and pepper; brush over chicken then place garlic cloves over and inside chicken.

3 Roast chicken 1-1/2 to 1-3/4 hours, or until golden and no pink remains, basting occasionally. Cut, and serve with pan juices.

TV Tidbit: I could never forget *this* recipe because, when the cameras rolled and I started to demonstrate my shortcut trick for peeling fresh garlic, those stubborn cloves kept slipping out of my hands and onto the floor! I won't tell you how many takes we shot 'til I got it right. Of course, my crew was in stitches the whole time!

Finger Lakes Company Chicken

Serves 4

1/2 cup Italian-seasoned bread crumbs

4 boneless, skinless chicken breast halves (about 1 pound)

4 thin slices Muenster cheese

1/4 cup dry white wine *or* 1/4 cup chicken broth

1 Preheat oven to 350°F. Coat an 8-inch square baking dish with nonstick cooking spray.

2 Place bread crumbs in a shallow dish. Dip chicken in bread crumbs coating well.

3 Place chicken in baking dish and bake 15 minutes. Remove chicken from oven and top each piece with a cheese slice; pour wine or broth evenly over top. Bake 15 more minutes, or until no pink remains in chicken and cheese is golden.

VIEWER FEEDBACK: At a book signing a few years ago, a very enthusiastic young lady came to tell me that her mother-in-law was always criticizing her cooking, but when she served this chicken dish after seeing me make it on TV, "Mom" couldn't stop praising her! She bought a copy of every one of my cookbooks in the store that day! (She said she'd try anything to get more compliments from her mother-in-law!)

Chicken & Biscuits

Serves 4 to 6

2 cups diced cooked chicken

1 (16-ounce) package frozen mixed vegetables

2 (12-ounce) jars chicken gravy

1 large (16.3-ounce) package refrigerated buttermilk biscuits (8 biscuits)

1 Preheat oven to 350°F. Coat a 9″ x 13″ baking dish with nonstick cooking spray.

2 In a large bowl, combine chicken, vegetables, and gravy; mix well then spoon into baking dish. Top with biscuits.

3 Bake 15 to 20 minutes, or until hot and bubbly, and the biscuits are golden.

TIMESAVING TIP: We're lucky we have options for buying pre-cooked chicken for recipes like these. We can use either cooked and diced packaged chicken, or dice it ourselves, using store-bought rotisserie chicken. Nobody has to know we did it without slaving in the kitchen for hours!

Pimiento Chicken

Serves 4

1/4 cup milk

1/4 cup Italian seasoned bread crumbs

4 boneless, skinless chicken breast halves (about 1 pound)

3 tablespoons butter

1 tablespoon olive oil

1/2 cup chicken broth

1 cup (1/2 pint) heavy cream

1 (4-ounce) jar diced pimientos, drained

1/2 cup grated Parmesan cheese

1/4 cup minced fresh basil

1/8 teaspoon black pepper

1 Place milk in a shallow dish and bread crumbs in another shallow dish. Dip chicken in milk then bread crumbs, turning to coat completely with each.

2 In a large skillet, melt butter with oil over medium heat. Add chicken and brown for 4 to 5 minutes per side, or until no pink remains in chicken. Remove chicken to a platter and cover to keep warm.

3 Add broth to skillet; bring to a boil over medium heat, scraping the browned bits from the bottom of the pan. Stir in heavy cream and pimientos. Bring to a boil and continue heating for about 1 minute, stirring constantly; reduce heat to medium-low.

4 Stir in Parmesan cheese, basil, and pepper, and cook until heated through. Slice chicken or serve whole, topped with sauce.

DID YOU KNOW...there's an incredibly easy trick for breading food without the usual mess? Simply use one hand to place food into the liquid (milk or beaten eggs), remove it with the same hand, place food into a shallow dish of dry breading mixture, and bread it with your other (dry) hand! One hand stays wet, one hand stays dry, and there are no more breaded fingers!

Potato Chip Chicken

Makes 18 to 20 pieces

1/3 cup milk

1 egg

1-1/4 cups (6-ounce bag) sour-cream-and-onion-flavored potato chips, finely crushed

1/4 teaspoon onion powder

1/4 teaspoon black pepper

3 boneless, skinless chicken breast halves, cut into 1-inch pieces

2 tablespoons butter, melted

1 Preheat oven to 400°F. Coat a rimmed baking pan with nonstick cooking spray.

2 In a small bowl, beat together milk and egg with a fork until well mixed. In a shallow dish, combine crushed potato chips, onion powder, and pepper.

3 Dip chicken pieces in egg mixture then roll them in potato chip mixture; repeat until all chicken is coated.

4 Arrange coated pieces in a single layer on baking pan; let sit at room temperature 15 minutes. Drizzle chicken with melted butter.

5 Bake 10 to 15 minutes, or until firm and golden.

SERVING TIP: Serve this up with ranch dressing as a dipping sauce, or maybe use your favorite potato chip dip! Talk about a fun recipe that everybody will love!

Twenty-Minute Italian Chili

Serves 6 to 8

1 pound boneless, skinless chicken thighs, cut into 1/2-inch chunks

1/2 pound Italian sausage, casings removed

1 medium onion, chopped

3 (14-1/2-ounce) cans Italian stewed tomatoes, undrained

2 (15-ounce) cans cannellini beans, undrained

2 tablespoons chili powder

1 teaspoon ground cumin

1/4 teaspoon salt

1 In a soup pot, cook chicken, sausage, and onion over high heat 5 to 6 minutes, or until browned, stirring to break up sausage.

2 Stir in remaining ingredients and bring to a boil. Reduce heat to medium and cook 15 minutes, stirring occasionally.

SERVING TIP: You've got to try my easy-as-can-be Cheese Twills to top this off. Get ready for raves when you serve it up!

Cheese Twills

Makes about 1 dozen pieces

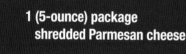

1 (5-ounce) package shredded Parmesan cheese

1 Preheat oven to 350°F. Coat a large rimmed baking sheet with nonstick cooking spray.

2 Sprinkle cheese over baking sheet, forming one large sheet of cheese. Bake 5 to 6 minutes, or until cheese is golden and melted.

3 Let cheese cool slightly then cut into triangles, squares, or rectangles. Or, make the shapes curved by forming them around or over a rolling pin, drinking glass, or bottom of a bowl while still warm. Let cool completely before using as desired.

Chicken Kiev Roll-Ups

Serves 6

2 tablespoons chopped fresh parsley

1 tablespoon dried chives

1/2 teaspoon garlic powder

6 boneless, skinless chicken breast halves, pounded to 1/4-inch thickness

1/2 teaspoon salt

1/2 teaspoon black pepper

3 tablespoons butter, cut into 6 equal slices

1 tablespoon seasoned bread crumbs

1/8 teaspoon paprika

1 Preheat oven to 350°F. Coat a 6-cup muffin tin with nonstick cooking spray.

2 In a small bowl, combine parsley, chives, and garlic powder; set aside.

3 Season both sides of each chicken breast with salt and pepper then lay breasts flat and sprinkle parsley mixture evenly over top of each.

4 Place a slice of butter in center of each breast and tightly roll up, tucking in sides as you roll. Place rolls seam-side down in muffin cups then sprinkle with bread crumbs and paprika.

5 Bake 25 to 30 minutes, or until no pink remains in chicken and juices run clear. Serve immediately.

TIMESAVING TIP: Muffin tins aren't just for cupcakes and muffins! They can save you cooking time with dishes like these chicken roll-ups and mini meat loaves, too! They're also perfect for making individual portions.

Mojito Chicken

Serves 6

3/4 cup fresh lime juice

1/2 cup light rum

1 teaspoon vegetable oil

1/3 cup fresh mint leaves, minced and loosely packed

1/4 cup sugar

1 teaspoon salt

6 boneless, skinless chicken breast halves

1 In a resealable plastic storage bag, combine all ingredients except chicken; mix well.

2 Add chicken breasts, and seal bag tightly after carefully squeezing out any excess air. Marinate in refrigerator 4 hours, turning occasionally.

3 Preheat grill to medium heat. Remove chicken from marinade, discarding marinade. Grill chicken 10 to 12 minutes per side, or until no pink remains and juices run clear.

SERVING TIP: I've got two tips for you! First, when you're grilling the chicken, grill some cut-up limes and use 'em as a garnish. Second, mix up some icy cold mojitos to have with this dish – it's a natural!

Stuffed Turkey Breast Dinner

Serves 4 to 6

1 (8-ounce) package herb
stuffing cubes

1/2 cup dried cranberries

1 (14-ounce) can
ready-to-serve
chicken broth

8 turkey breast cutlets
(about 2 pounds total)

2 (12-ounce) jars
turkey gravy

1 Preheat oven to 350°F. Coat a 9" x 13" baking dish with nonstick cooking spray.

2 In a large bowl, combine stuffing, dried cranberries, and broth; mix well.

3 Place turkey cutlets on a work surface and place an equal amount of stuffing mixture in the center of each. Roll up each cutlet and place seam-side down in baking dish.

4 Pour gravy over roll-ups. Cover and bake 35 to 40 minutes, or until cooked through and no pink remains in turkey.

VIEWER FEEDBACK: I had to laugh when a viewer emailed to tell me she'll never cook and talk on the phone at the same time again. When she made this, she mistakenly grabbed a package of chopped sun-dried tomatoes from her pantry, instead of dried cranberries. Of course, when she tasted it, she figured out what happened…and she started all over!

Beer Can Chicken

Serves 4

1/2 cup barbecue sauce

1 (12-ounce) can beer, half full (see Options)

1 tablespoon dried basil

2 teaspoons paprika

1/2 teaspoon onion powder

1/4 teaspoon garlic powder

3/4 teaspoon salt

1/4 teaspoon black pepper

1 (3- to 3-1/2-pound) whole chicken

1 Preheat grill to medium-high heat. Add barbecue sauce to half-full can of beer.

2 In a small bowl, combine basil, paprika, onion powder, garlic powder, salt, and pepper; mix well and rub evenly over chicken.

3 Place cavity of chicken over beer can so chicken is sitting on can then place can (with chicken on it) on rack in center of grill. Cover grill and cook chicken 1 to 1-1/4 hours, or until no pink remains and juices run clear.

4 Carefully pour remaining sauce from can into a bowl, and serve with chicken.

OPTIONS: This can also be made with nonalcoholic beer or, for a different flavor, you could use a half-filled can of lemonade and rub the chicken with lemon-pepper seasoning. Cooking time will vary depending upon the grill used.

TV Tidbit: On the day we taped this show, the chicken just wouldn't cooperate. Every time I set it on that beer can, it tipped over. I was tempted to call it "Drunken Chicken."

Mouthwatering Meats

Kung Pao Beef

Serves 6 to 8

1/2 cup teriyaki sauce

2 tablespoons cornstarch

1 teaspoon crushed
red pepper

1/2 teaspoon ground ginger

1 (2-pound) flank steak,
thinly sliced

1 tablespoon vegetable oil

2/3 cup salted peanuts

4 scallions, thinly sliced

1 In a large bowl, combine teriyaki sauce, cornstarch, red pepper, and ginger. Add flank steak and toss to coat.

2 In a large skillet, heat oil over high heat. Add steak mixture and cook 5 to 7 minutes, or until steak is cooked through, stirring constantly.

3 Sprinkle with peanuts and scallions, and serve.

SERVING TIP: Break out the chopsticks and serve this Asian specialty over a bed of basmati rice or Chinese rice noodles for a flavor-packed change-of-pace main course.

Chicken-Fried Steak

Serves 4

1/3 cup plus 1 tablespoon all-purpose flour, divided

3/4 teaspoon salt, divided

1/2 teaspoon pepper, divided

2 large eggs, beaten

1 tablespoon water

1-1/2 cups plain bread crumbs

4 (4-ounce) cubed steaks

5 tablespoons butter, divided

1 cup milk

1 In a shallow dish, combine 1/3 cup flour, 1/2 teaspoon salt, and 1/4 teaspoon pepper. In another shallow dish, combine the eggs and water. Place bread crumbs in a third shallow dish.

2 Coat steaks with flour mixture then dip in egg mixture and coat with bread crumbs.

3 In a large nonstick skillet, melt 4 tablespoons butter over medium heat. Add steaks, and fry 3 to 4 minutes per side, or until cooked through and golden. Drain on a paper towel-lined platter and cover to keep warm.

4 Make a white gravy by adding the remaining 1 tablespoon butter to skillet and melting over low heat; add remaining 1 tablespoon flour, and stir until smooth. Cook 1 minute, stirring constantly. Gradually add milk; cook over medium heat until thickened and bubbly, stirring constantly. Stir in remaining 1/4 teaspoon salt and 1/4 teaspoon pepper. Serve steaks topped with gravy.

DID YOU KNOW...this down-home dish has its roots in the South and Midwest? The story goes that it was originally made by folks looking for ways to use their tougher beef cuts, the ones that, these days, are less expensive. I'm all for anything that saves us money and tastes this good, aren't you?

Margarita Steak

Serves 4

1 (12-ounce) can frozen margarita mix

4 boneless beef strip or chuck shoulder steaks, cut 3/4-inch thick (about 2 pounds total)

1 teaspoon coarse (kosher) salt

1 Place margarita mix in a large resealable plastic storage bag; add steaks, seal, and marinate in refrigerator at least 2 hours.

2 Preheat grill to medium heat; grill steaks 2 to 3 minutes per side for medium, or until desired doneness.

3 Remove steaks from grill and sprinkle evenly with coarse salt before serving.

SERVING TIP: What could possibly make these steaks more exciting? I like to add more zip by topping them with chopped cilantro and fresh jalapeño peppers!

Muffin Tin Meat Loaves

Makes 12 muffins

1-1/2 pounds lean ground beef

1 egg, slightly beaten

1-1/2 cups shredded (about 1 medium) zucchini

1 teaspoon dried Italian seasoning

1/2 teaspoon salt

1 cup bread crumbs

1/4 cup ketchup

1 Preheat oven to 400°F.

2 In a large bowl, combine all ingredients except ketchup, mixing lightly but thoroughly. Place about 1/3 cup beef mixture into each of 12 medium muffin cups, pressing lightly; spread ketchup over tops.

3 Bake 20 minutes, or until no pink remains and juices run clear.

TIMESAVING TIP: These cook up almost twice as fast as traditional meat loaves since they're made in individual portions. They're easy, fast and, of course..."OOH IT'S SO GOOD!!®"

Not-Rolled Rolled Cabbage

Serves 8

1-1/4 pounds ground beef

1/2 cup plain bread crumbs

1 egg

1 teaspoon salt

1/4 teaspoon pepper

1 medium head green
cabbage, shredded
(12 to 14 cups)

1 (16-ounce) can jellied or
whole-berry cranberry sauce

5 gingersnap cookies,
crumbled (about 1/4 cup
crumbs)

1 tablespoon lemon juice

1 (28-ounce) jar
spaghetti sauce

1 In a medium bowl, combine ground beef, bread crumbs, egg, salt, and pepper. Form mixture into 1-inch meatballs (about 1 tablespoon each).

2 Place half the shredded cabbage in a soup pot then add the meatballs. Spread cranberry sauce over meatballs, sprinkle with gingersnap crumbs and lemon juice then add remaining cabbage. Pour spaghetti sauce over mixture and do not stir.

3 Bring to a boil then reduce heat to low; simmer uncovered for 20 minutes. Stir gently, being careful not to break up meatballs. Simmer for another 40 minutes, stirring halfway through.

NOTE: If you like your rolled cabbage on the sweeter side, add a tablespoon or two of dark brown sugar to the spaghetti sauce before pouring that over the cabbage.

VIEWER FEEDBACK: This show generated a load of thank-you emails from viewers. The idea for this shortcut version actually came from my wife Ethel ("Mrs. Food"), who's a great cook herself, so I "shared the love" from all of you with her. We sure do make a great team!

Hula Sliders

Serves 6

1/2 cup mayonnaise

1/4 cup plus 2 tablespoons pineapple preserves

1/8 teaspoon plus 1/2 teaspoon salt

1-1/4 pounds ground beef

1/4 teaspoon onion powder

1/4 teaspoon pepper

6 slices pepper-Jack cheese, each cut into quarters

1 (12-count) package Hawaiian bread rolls *or* slider rolls

1 In a small bowl, combine mayonnaise, 1/4 cup pineapple preserves, and 1/8 teaspoon salt; mix well then refrigerate until ready to use.

2 Preheat grill to medium-high heat. In a medium bowl, combine ground beef, remaining 2 tablespoons preserves, the onion powder, remaining 1/2 teaspoon salt, and 1/4 teaspoon pepper; mix well then divide mixture into 12 equal amounts and make 12 patties.

3 Grill patties 4 to 6 minutes, or until desired doneness, turning them over halfway through grilling.

4 Place 2 pieces of cheese on each slider about 2 minutes before burgers are finished cooking. Place each slider on a toasted sweet roll and top with pineapple mayonnaise sauce.

SERVING SUGGESTION: Try serving these with grilled pineapple. Just slice a fresh pineapple in half lengthwise then cut into 4" slices and grill slices a couple minutes per side.

Bread Bowl Chili

Serves 8

2 pounds ground beef

1 teaspoon minced garlic

1 (28-ounce) can crushed tomatoes

2 (15-ounce) cans red kidney beans, undrained

1 (1-ounce) envelope onion soup mix

3 tablespoons chili powder

8 kaiser rolls

1 In a large pot, combine ground beef and garlic over medium-high heat and brown for 10 minutes.

2 Add crushed tomatoes, kidney beans, soup mix, and chili powder; mix well and bring to a boil, stirring frequently. Reduce heat to low and simmer 30 minutes.

3 Meanwhile, cut the very top off each roll and remove the insides, creating bowls.

4 Place bread bowls on plates and spoon chili into them, allowing chili to overflow.

SERVING TIP: Make sure to have all the traditional go-alongs like sour cream, chopped onions, and shredded cheese on hand to use as chili toppers.

Diner Salisbury Steak

Serves 4

1-1/2 pounds ground beef

2 scallions, finely chopped

1/4 cup Italian-seasoned bread crumbs

1 egg

1 tablespoon yellow mustard

1 (12-ounce) container beef gravy

1/2 cup water

2 teaspoons prepared white horseradish

1/2 pound fresh mushrooms, thinly sliced

1 Coat a large skillet with nonstick cooking spray.

2 In a medium bowl, combine ground beef, scallions, bread crumbs, egg, and mustard; mix well. Shape into four 1/2-inch-thick oval patties.

3 Heat skillet over medium-high heat and cook patties 3 to 4 minutes per side, or until no pink remains.

4 Add gravy, water, horseradish, and mushrooms, and cook 4 to 5 minutes, or until mushrooms are tender, stirring occasionally.

NOTE: Each patty makes a hearty serving, so you can certainly make smaller portions — just form the mixture into 6 or 8 smaller patties and adjust the cooking time, if necessary.

TV Tidbit: This recipe brings back memories of a series we did some years ago from a local diner. Not only was it a blast to taste this "blue plate special" along with creamy shakes and mile-high pies, but we learned a lot of fun diner lingo that day, too, like a "white cow" is a vanilla milkshake and a "chocolate cow" is...you guessed it: a chocolate milkshake!

Beef & Guinness Casserole

Serves 4 to 6

3 slices raw bacon, chopped

1 tablespoon vegetable oil

2 pounds beef stew meat

1-1/2 cups (12 ounces)
Guinness beer

3 cups beef stock

2 cloves garlic, minced

1/2 teaspoon salt

1/2 teaspoon black pepper

12 ounces baby carrots

4 celery stalks, sliced into
1/2-inch chunks

1 large yellow onion, peeled
and cut into half-moons

1 to 2 tablespoons all-
purpose flour

1/3 cup water

1 Place bacon in a heavy soup pot or Dutch oven and cook over high heat until crisp. Stir in oil and stew meat, and continue cooking for 8 to 10 minutes, or until meat is browned.

2 Stir in beer, beef stock, garlic, salt, and pepper; reduce heat to low, and simmer, covered, for 30 minutes.

3 Add carrots, celery, and onion; stir well, cover and cook 1 hour, or until meat is tender.

4 Mix flour with water then stir into stew. Cook 1 to 2 minutes, or until sauce is thickened.

TV Tidbit: One of my most unforgettable series shoots took me on location all around western Ireland. It was quite an experience learning how to pour a Guinness at a traditional Irish pub, where we also enjoyed this succulent Beef & Guinness Casserole. I hope you caught my Ireland series on TV or online, and I hope you give this dish a try at home!

Spicy Orange Beef

Serves 4

3 tablespoons peanut oil, divided

1 tablespoon soy sauce

1 teaspoon ground ginger

1/2 teaspoon sugar

1 to 1-1/2 pounds beef top or bottom round steak, cut into 2-inch strips

Peel of 1 orange, cut into 1/8-inch strips

2 tablespoons all-purpose flour

1/4 cup orange juice

1/4 teaspoon ground red pepper

1/2 cup ready-to-serve beef broth

1 In a medium bowl, combine 1 tablespoon peanut oil, the soy sauce, ginger, and sugar; mix well. Add beef strips and toss to coat.

2 Meanwhile, in a large skillet or wok, heat remaining peanut oil over medium heat. Add orange peel to skillet and sauté 3 to 4 minutes, or until it begins to brown.

3 Add flour to meat mixture and stir until well coated; place beef in skillet and cook 5 to 7 minutes, or until no pink remains, stirring occasionally.

4 Add orange juice, ground red pepper, and beef broth. Stir well to mix any flour from bottom of pan. Reduce heat to low and cook 7 to 9 more minutes, or until sauce is thickened.

SERVING TIP: This is great served as is or over plain or fried rice.

Cola Roast

Serves 8 to 10

1 teaspoon salt

1/2 teaspoon black pepper

1/2 teaspoon garlic powder

1 (4- to 5-pound) beef bottom round roast

3 tablespoons vegetable oil

12 ounces carbonated cola beverage

1 (12-ounce) bottle chili sauce

2 tablespoons Worcestershire sauce

2 tablespoons hot pepper sauce

1 Preheat oven to 325°F. Coat a roasting pan with nonstick cooking spray.

2 In a small bowl, combine salt, black pepper, and garlic powder; mix well then rub over surface of roast.

3 In a soup pot, heat oil over medium-high heat and brown roast on all sides. Transfer roast to roasting pan.

4 In a medium bowl, combine remaining ingredients; mix well then pour over roast. Cover with aluminum foil and roast 2-1/2 to 3 hours, or until meat is fork-tender.

HEALTHY HINT: Any kind of cola works fine here. If you prefer to skip regular, go for diet or caffeine-free and the roast will still pick up all the cola flavor. Another tip? Use canola or another light oil in place of vegetable oil for browning the roast.

Crowd-Pleasing Brisket

Serves 10 to 12

1 (4- to 4-1/2-pound) fresh
brisket of beef

2-1/2 cups ketchup

3/4 cup prepared mustard

1 cup packed brown sugar

1/2 cup water

1 Preheat oven to 350°F. Coat a large roasting pan with nonstick cooking spray and place brisket in roasting pan.

2 In a large bowl, combine ketchup, mustard, and brown sugar. Remove 1 cup of sauce to a medium bowl and add the water to it; mix well and pour around meat in pan. Pour remaining sauce over top of meat, making sure some of it stays on top. Cover tightly with aluminum foil.

3 Bake 3 to 3-1/2 hours, or until meat is fork-tender. Slice across the grain and serve with sauce over the top.

TIMESAVING TIP: Long-cooked dishes like this one really benefit when you use a make-ahead, timesaving strategy for dinner or entertaining. Extra overnight fridge time allows the flavors to fully seep into the meat, rewarding our taste buds with even richer flavor.

Dinosaur Ribs

Serves 4 to 6

1 tablespoon ground cumin

1 tablespoon dried oregano

1 tablespoon dried thyme

1 tablespoon chili powder

1 tablespoon garlic powder

1 teaspoon salt

6 to 7 pounds beef back ribs, trimmed and cut into individual ribs

1/4 cup barbecue sauce

1 Preheat oven to 375°F. Line a large roasting pan with aluminum foil then place a roasting rack in pan. Coat rack with nonstick cooking spray.

2 In a small bowl, combine cumin, oregano, thyme, chili powder, garlic powder, and salt; mix well then rub seasoning mixture evenly over ribs. Place ribs on roasting rack, overlapping if necessary.

3 Roast uncovered for 1 hour.

4 Brush ribs with barbecue sauce and roast uncovered for 25 to 30 more minutes, or until tender and cooked through. Serve immediately.

SERVING TIP: Try serving these larger-than-life hearty ribs the way I do, with plenty of additional barbecue sauce on the side. And make sure you've got plenty of napkins ready!

Skillet Corned Beef & Cabbage

Serves 4 to 6

2 tablespoons vegetable or canola oil

8 cups chunked, green cabbage (1/2 large head)

1/2 teaspoon salt

1/4 teaspoon black pepper

2 (15-ounce) cans whole potatoes, drained (see Note)

1 (14-1/2-ounce) can sliced carrots, drained

3/4 pound deli-style corned beef, sliced into 1/2-inch strips

1 In a large skillet, heat oil over medium heat. Add cabbage, and sauté 6 to 8 minutes, until very soft but not brown. Add salt and pepper; mix well.

2 Add potatoes and carrots, and top with corned beef. Reduce heat to medium-low, cover, and cook 6 to 8 minutes, or until completely heated through. Serve immediately.

NOTE: I like to rinse my canned potatoes and drain them well before using.

TV Tidbit: This classic Irish dish always reminds me of the fun I have appearing in the annual St. Patrick's Day parade in Chicago. I just love sharing the big celebration from the WLS-TV float!

Valentine's Veal

Serves 4

1/4 cup all-purpose flour

1 egg, beaten

1 pound veal cutlets, pounded to 1/4-inch thickness

2 tablespoons butter

1 (14-ounce) can artichokes, drained and chopped

1/4 cup sun-dried tomatoes, reconstituted and chopped

1/3 cup dry vermouth *or* white wine

3 tablespoons lemon juice

1 Place flour and egg in separate shallow dishes. Coat veal with flour then egg.

2 In a large skillet, melt butter over medium heat. Cook veal in batches for 2 to 3 minutes per side, or until golden.

3 Stir in artichokes, sun-dried tomatoes, vermouth, and lemon juice. Cook 2 to 3 minutes, or until sauce thickens. Serve immediately.

SERVING TIP: I hope you'll enjoy this restaurant-worthy dish year-round, but when you make it for your Valentine, be sure to team it with colorful, healthy Beet Mashed Potatoes.

Beet Mashed Potatoes

Serves 8

6 medium potatoes (about 2 pounds), peeled and cut into chunks

1 (15-ounce) can beets, undrained

1/4 cup (1/2 stick) butter, softened

1/4 teaspoon onion powder

1/2 teaspoon salt

1/2 teaspoon black pepper

1 Place potatoes in a soup pot and add just enough water to cover them. Add beets and their liquid, and bring to a boil over high heat. Reduce heat to medium and cook 12 to 15 minutes, or until potatoes are fork-tender.

2 Drain potatoes and place in a large bowl. Add remaining ingredients and beat with an electric beater on medium speed until well blended. Serve immediately; cover and refrigerate any leftovers.

Greek Lamb Kebabs

Makes 30 to 35 medium-sized kebabs

30 to 35 (6- to 8-inch) wooden or metal skewers

2-1/2 pounds ground lamb

3/4 cup minced onion

1/2 cup chopped fresh parsley

1/4 cup tomato sauce

1 teaspoon salt

1/2 teaspoon black pepper

1 If using wooden skewers, soak them in water for 15 to 20 minutes.

2 Preheat broiler to high.

3 In a large bowl, combine all ingredients; mix well. Roll mixture into 30 to 35 sausage-like shapes and place on 2 broiler pans or rimmed baking sheets. Place one skewer into the end of each lamb roll.

NOTE: If you want to cook these on the grill, that works, too! Just place the skewers crosswise on the grill rack, on a preheated grill, and cook as directed.

4 Broil 5 to 7 minutes per side, turning once, until cooked through. Serve as is or with my Feta Cheese Dipping Sauce.

Feta Cheese Dipping Sauce

Makes 3 cups

8 ounces feta cheese

1 cup plain yogurt

1 cup sour cream

1 large cucumber, peeled and cut into chunks

4 cloves garlic

1-1/2 teaspoons dried mint

3 tablespoons olive oil

4 teaspoons red wine vinegar

1/2 teaspoon salt

1/2 teaspoon onion powder

1 In a food processor or blender, blend all ingredients until smooth. Serve immediately, or place in a medium bowl, cover, and chill until ready to use.

Secret Glazed Spareribs

Serves 4 to 6

4 to 5 pounds pork spareribs

3/4 cup bottled chili sauce

1/2 cup grape jelly

2 teaspoons dry mustard

1 Place ribs in a large soup pot and cover with water. Cover pot and boil 45 minutes to 1 hour, until tender.

2 Preheat grill to medium-high heat about 10 minutes before ribs finish boiling.

3 Meanwhile, in a medium bowl, combine remaining ingredients.

4 Place ribs on grill and close grill lid. Grill ribs about 12 to 15 minutes, or until browned and glazed, turning them over frequently and basting with sauce mixture each time they are turned.

VIEWER FEEDBACK: I can't tell you how often I'm told that these are the "best ribs ever!" Whether it's by email or in my travels around the country, viewers are always raving that this recipe is a real crowd-pleaser!

Cheesy Baked Pork Chops

Serves 4

1 cup finely crushed cheese crackers

1/4 cup sesame seeds

1 tablespoon chopped fresh parsley

1/2 teaspoon salt

1/4 teaspoon black pepper

1/4 teaspoon ground red pepper

2 eggs

4 (1-inch) pork loin chops (1-1/4 to 1-1/2 pounds total)

Nonstick cooking spray

1 Preheat oven to 400°F. Coat a rimmed baking sheet with nonstick cooking spray.

2 In a shallow bowl, combine cracker crumbs, sesame seeds, parsley, salt, black and red peppers; mix well. Beat eggs in another shallow bowl.

3 Dip each pork chop into the eggs then seasoned crumbs, coating well. Place chops on baking sheet.

4 Spray both sides of chops with nonstick cooking spray then bake 40 to 45 minutes for medium, or to desired doneness beyond that, turning halfway through cooking.

SERVING TIP: Although these juicy, cheesy pork chops can truly pair with anything, my vote is always for some fluffy mashed potatoes!

Jammin' Pork

Serves 6 to 8

1/4 cup honey

1/3 cup lime juice

1 teaspoon grated lime peel

2 garlic cloves, minced

2 tablespoons yellow mustard

1/2 teaspoon salt

1/2 teaspoon black pepper

2 pork tenderloins (2 pounds total), well trimmed

1 In a large resealable plastic storage bag, combine all ingredients except tenderloins; mix well. Add tenderloins, seal, and marinate in refrigerator at least 4 hours, or overnight, turning bag occasionally.

2 Preheat broiler.

3 Place pork on a broiler pan or rimmed baking sheet; discard marinade. Broil 7 to 9 minutes per side, or until desired doneness.

4 Slice tenderloins across the grain and serve.

HEALTHY HINT: Pork tenderloin is one of the leanest cuts available at the supermarket meat department. If trimmed, a single portion has only 1 gram of saturated fat. That's why it's such a healthy choice!

Peachy Pork Tenderloin

Serves 6

1 cup peach preserves

1/4 cup white vinegar

2 tablespoons Dijon mustard

2 tablespoons vegetable oil

2 pork tenderloins (about 2 pounds total)

1/4 teaspoon salt

1/4 teaspoon black pepper

2 cups fresh peach slices *or* frozen peach slices, thawed

1 In a small bowl, stir together preserves, vinegar, and mustard; set aside.

2 In a large skillet, heat oil over medium-high heat. Season tenderloins with salt and pepper, and add to skillet. Cook 4 to 5 minutes, turning to brown on all sides.

3 Reduce heat to medium-low and add reserved preserves mixture. Cover and simmer 18 to 20 minutes, until pork is only slightly pink in center and internal temperature reaches 160°F. for medium, or to desired doneness beyond that.

4 Add peaches and cook until heated through. Slice and serve topped with peach sauce.

SERVING TIP: Serve warm slices of tenderloin over mixed salad greens. Top it with peach sauce and garnish with fresh raspberries for the exciting contrast of hot and cold, savory and sweet.

Anytime Ham

Serves 10 to 12

1 (4- to 5-pound) smoked
semi-boneless ham

1 (29-ounce) can yams,
drained

2 (15-ounce) cans whole
white potatoes, drained

1 (29-ounce) can peach
halves in heavy syrup,
drained and syrup reserved

1 (16-ounce) can apricot
halves in heavy syrup,
drained and syrup reserved

3/4 cup maple syrup

1 teaspoon dry mustard

1/8 teaspoon ground ginger

3 tablespoons cornstarch

1 Preheat oven to 400°F. Trim ham of all excess fat and place cut-side down in a large roasting pan. Bake 45 minutes then drain off any pan drippings and reduce heat to 350°F.

2 Meanwhile, place yams, white potatoes, peaches, and apricots in a large bowl and toss gently; set aside.

3 In a medium saucepan, combine 1 cup reserved peach syrup, 1/2 cup reserved apricot syrup, the maple syrup, dry mustard, and ginger; bring to a boil over medium-high heat then remove from heat.

4 In a small bowl, mix 3 tablespoons of the remaining reserved apricot or peach syrup with cornstarch and add to hot syrup mixture, stirring until thickened. Place potatoes and fruit around ham and pour syrup mixture over everything.

5 Bake 35 to 45 minutes, uncovered, basting occasionally, until ham is heated through.

NOTE: Carve ham across the grain and, don't forget, if there's anything left over, it's ideal for sandwiches or homemade hash.

Creamy Basil Pork Chops

Serves 6

3 tablespoons olive oil, divided

4 garlic cloves, minced

6 (1/2-inch-thick) pork loin chops (2 pounds total), well trimmed

2 tablespoons chopped fresh basil

1/4 teaspoon salt

1/4 teaspoon black pepper

1/3 cup heavy cream

1 In a large skillet, heat 2 tablespoons olive oil over medium-high heat. Add the garlic, and sauté 1 to 2 minutes. Reduce heat to medium, add pork chops, and cook 6 to 7 minutes per side, until brown on both sides.

2 Meanwhile, in a small bowl, combine remaining 1 tablespoon olive oil, the basil, salt, and pepper; add to skillet 3 to 4 minutes before chops are done, spreading mixture around skillet and turning chops to coat with basil mixture. When chops are cooked through, remove to a serving plate and cover to keep warm.

3 Whisk cream into pan drippings for 2 to 3 minutes over medium heat, until sauce thickens slightly. Pour sauce over cooked chops and serve immediately.

ROASTED PLUM TOMATOES make a perfect go-along: In a large bowl, combine 2 tablespoons vegetable oil, 1 teaspoon salt, 1/4 teaspoon black pepper, 1/4 teaspoon garlic powder, 1/4 teaspoon onion powder. Cut 12 plum tomatoes in half lengthwise and gently squeeze out the seeds and juice. Toss in oil mixture then pour into a 9" x 13" baking dish. Roast 20 to 25 minutes in a preheated 450°F. oven until tender but not overcooked. Sprinkle with 2 tablespoons chopped fresh basil, and serve. Serves 6.

Tropical Pork Kebabs

Serves 8

8 wooden or metal skewers

2 pounds pork loin, cut into 1-inch chunks

2 large red bell peppers, cored, cleaned, and cut into 8 pieces each

1 large green bell pepper, cored, cleaned, and cut into 8 pieces

1/2 fresh pineapple, cut into 4 slices then into 1/4-inch wedges

1/2 cup honey

1/2 cup lime juice

2 teaspoons grated lime peel

3 garlic cloves, minced

1/4 cup yellow mustard

1 teaspoon salt

3/4 teaspoon black pepper

1 If using wooden skewers, soak them in water for 15 to 20 minutes.

2 Alternately thread each skewer with pork chunks, 2 red pepper pieces, 1 green pepper piece, and 2 pineapple wedges.

3 In a 9" x 13" baking dish, combine honey, lime juice, grated lime peel, garlic, mustard, salt, and black pepper; mix well. Place kebabs in baking dish and rotate to coat with marinade. Cover and refrigerate at least 4 hours or overnight, turning occasionally.

4 Preheat grill to medium-high heat.

5 Baste kebabs with marinade; discard excess marinade. Grill kebabs 7 to 9 minutes, or until no pink remains in pork, turning frequently to cook on all sides.

TV Tidbit: This succulent dish was featured on a segment I'll never forget…and neither will my crew! We were shooting in a park on a perfect day. As the cameras starting rolling, the park's sprinklers began shooting, too! Yup, we all got drenched in a matter of seconds! Luckily, the park ranger got the sprinklers turned off pronto while we dried off and started over. Don't I lead a glamorous life?!

Fast Fish & Seafood

Lemonade Poached Salmon

Serves 4

1 cup mayonnaise

1 (12-ounce) can frozen lemonade concentrate, thawed, divided

1/4 teaspoon black pepper

1/4 cup water

4 salmon fillets (about 1-1/2 pounds total)

1 In a small bowl, combine mayonnaise, 3 tablespoons lemonade concentrate, and the pepper; mix well then cover and chill.

2 In a large skillet, combine remaining lemonade concentrate and the water; bring to a boil over medium-low heat. Add salmon and reduce heat to low; cover, and cook 8 to 10 minutes, or until fish flakes easily with a fork.

3 Allow salmon to cool to room temperature and serve with chilled lemonade sauce.

SERVING SUGGESTION: This can be made in advance and served well chilled for a refreshing light lunch. To give it extra color and flair, garnish each serving with a sprig of fresh dill and a slice of lemon.

HEALTHY HINT: Few foods are as nutritious as salmon. Even though it's considered a fatty fish, its fat is good for us, because omega-3 fatty acids promote cardiovascular health. Salmon is also packed with protein and virtually devoid of carbohydrates. When we make it with a healthy cooking method like poaching, we can't beat salmon's benefits!

Golden-Topped Salmon

Serves 4

1/3 cup mayonnaise

1 tablespoon fresh
lemon juice

1 garlic clove, minced

1 tablespoon fresh
chopped dill (see note)

1/4 teaspoon salt

1/4 teaspoon black pepper

4 (6-ounce) salmon fillets

1 Preheat broiler. Coat a broiler pan or rimmed baking sheet with nonstick cooking spray.

2 In a small bowl, combine all ingredients except salmon; mix well.

3 Place salmon fillets on baking sheet; spread mayonnaise mixture evenly over the top of the salmon.

4 Broil salmon 10 to 12 minutes, or until it flakes easily with a fork. Serve immediately.

SERVING TIP: I like to sauté a bag of fresh baby spinach with some fresh garlic in a bit of olive oil for a minute or two and serve the salmon on a bed of wilted spinach.

DID YOU KNOW...
1 tablespoon of fresh chopped dill equals 1 teaspoon of dried?

Salmon Fingers

Makes 6 to 8 strips

1/2 cup finely crushed Cap'n Crunch® cereal

1/4 cup finely crushed butter-flavored crackers

1/4 cup finely chopped pistachio nuts

Nonstick cooking spray

1 pound salmon fillets, skin removed and cut into "fingers" (strips)

1 Preheat oven to 350°F. Coat a rimmed baking sheet with nonstick cooking spray.

2 In a shallow dish, combine cereal, crackers, and nuts; mix well.

3 Lightly coat salmon fingers with nonstick cooking spray then dip in cereal mixture, coating completely. Place on baking sheet and lightly coat with cooking spray.

4 Bake 10 to 12 minutes, or until fish flakes easily with a fork.

TV Tidbit: One of my chef friends, Carmine Sprio, from Albany, New York, graciously shared this recipe with me and my viewers. When we taped this show together, I had a hunch we had a winner, and when we were overwhelmed by requests for the recipe, my hunch was confirmed!

Sesame Tuna

Serves 2

1/4 cup soy sauce

3 teaspoons wasabi paste (see below)

1/2 teaspoon cracked black pepper

2 (6-ounce) 3/4-inch-thick ahi tuna steaks

1/4 cup sesame seeds

1 In a shallow dish, combine soy sauce, wasabi paste, and cracked black pepper; mix well. Add tuna and turn until thoroughly coated on both sides; let sit for 10 minutes.

2 Coat a grill pan with nonstick cooking spray and preheat over high heat.

3 Place sesame seeds in another shallow dish, add tuna and turn to coat completely.

4 Grill tuna 1 to 2 minutes per side, or until browned outside and cooked to desired doneness. Be careful not to overcook it! Slice thinly and serve.

DID YOU KNOW...wasabi is Japanese horseradish? It's usually served in paste form as a condiment for sushi and sashimi. Since Japanese food, particularly sushi, has become so popular all across the U.S., we can now find wasabi paste in most supermarkets.

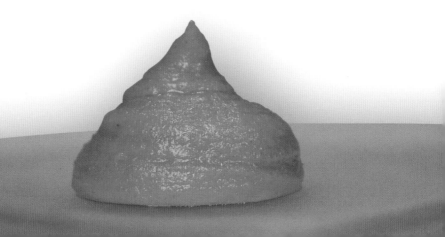

Blackened Grouper

Serves 4

2 tablespoons paprika

1 teaspoon crushed
   dried thyme

1/2 teaspoon onion powder

1/2 teaspoon garlic powder

1/2 teaspoon sugar

1/4 teaspoon ground
   red pepper

1/2 teaspoon salt

1/2 teaspoon black pepper

4 (5- to 6-ounce) grouper
   fillets

1 Spray cold barbecue grill racks with nonstick cooking spray. Preheat grill to medium-high heat.

2 In a small bowl, combine paprika, thyme, onion powder, garlic powder, sugar, red pepper, salt, and black pepper; mix well. Rub evenly over both sides of fish.

3 Grill fish 7 to 8 minutes per side, or until it is cooked through and flakes easily with a fork.

OPTIONS: This is a really flavor-packed dish, and it's versatile, too. You can substitute almost any fish for the grouper. Try this with all your favorites!

Clams Pomodoro

Serves 4

2 dozen clams

1 (14-1/2-ounce) can stewed tomatoes, chopped, with juice reserved

1/4 cup dry white wine

2 tablespoons chopped fresh basil

1/4 teaspoon black pepper

1 In a large soup pot, combine all ingredients, including reserved stewed tomato juice.

2 Cover and bring to a boil over high heat; reduce heat to low and simmer 6 to 8 minutes, or until clams open. Do not overcook. Discard any clams that do not open.

3 Remove to a serving bowl or individual bowls, and serve.

DID YOU KNOW...a clam should not be eaten if its shell is still tightly closed after cooking? The shell should open widely on its own during cooking. If it doesn't...be safe and toss it!

Almond-Crusted Flounder

Serves 4

1 tablespoon sugar

3/4 teaspoon ground cinnamon

1/4 teaspoon ground red pepper

1/2 teaspoon salt

1-1/2 pounds flounder fillets

1 egg white, beaten

2 cups sliced almonds

2 tablespoons butter, plus more as needed

1/4 cup olive oil, plus more as needed

1/2 cup amaretto liqueur

1 In a small bowl, combine sugar, cinnamon, red pepper, and salt; mix well. Season fillets with 1 teaspoon of the mixture, reserving remaining mixture.

2 Place egg white in a shallow dish; place almonds in another shallow dish. Dip each fillet in egg white then almonds, coating completely.

3 In a large skillet, melt butter with oil over medium heat. Add half the fillets and cook 5 minutes then turn fillets and cook 2 to 3 more minutes, or until fish flakes easily with a fork; transfer to a serving platter and cover to keep warm. Repeat with remaining fillets, adding additional butter and oil as needed.

4 Add reserved sugar mixture and amaretto to skillet; reduce heat to low and cook 1 to 2 minutes, or until thickened, stirring constantly. Pour over fillets and serve immediately.

SERVING TIP: Pair this with some wild rice tossed with a bit of grated orange peel. You'll have 'em saying, "Ooh la la!"

Mango Tango Fillets

Serves 6

1 medium mango, peeled, pitted, and diced

1 red bell pepper, diced

1/2 small red onion, diced

1 (8-1/4-ounce) can pineapple tidbits, drained, with juice reserved

1/4 teaspoon salt, divided

1/2 teaspoon ground red pepper, divided

6 white-fleshed fish fillets (2 pounds total), such as cod, orange roughy, or flounder

1/2 cup water

1 In a medium bowl, combine mango, bell pepper, onion, pineapple, 1/8 teaspoon salt, and 1/4 teaspoon ground red pepper; mix well, cover, and chill.

2 Place fish in a large skillet and pour reserved pineapple juice along with 1/2 cup water over it. Sprinkle fish with remaining 1/8 teaspoon salt and 1/4 teaspoon ground red pepper.

3 Cover fish and bring liquid to a boil over high heat. Reduce heat to low and cook 7 to 8 minutes, or until fish flakes easily with a fork. Serve immediately, topped with chilled mango salsa.

SERVING TIP: I like to serve this garnished with finely chopped fresh cilantro.

DID YOU KNOW...mangoes are the most popular fruit in the world, with more than 2000 different varieties? I'm lucky to have a few mango trees in my yard and, during mango season, I can't stop eating them! Mangoes aren't nearly as popular in America as in other parts of the world, but this recipe sure shows them off, so pick up a mango (or two) today.

Oven-"Fried" Fish

Serves 4 to 6

2 egg whites, beaten

1 tablespoon lemon juice

1 teaspoon dried dill weed

1/2 teaspoon salt

1 teaspoon black pepper

1 cup cornflake crumbs

2 pounds fresh or frozen white-fleshed fish fillets, such as cod, haddock, or whiting, thawed if frozen

Nonstick cooking spray

1 Preheat oven to 400°F. Coat a baking sheet with nonstick cooking spray.

2 In a shallow dish, combine egg whites, lemon juice, dill weed, salt, and pepper. Place cornflake crumbs in another shallow dish.

3 Dip fish in egg mixture then crumbs, coating evenly; place on a baking sheet. Lightly spray fish with nonstick cooking spray.

4 Bake 10 to 12 minutes, or until fish flakes easily with a fork.

VIEWER FEEDBACK: Irene from St. Louis, Missouri, wrote to me after this recipe aired: "I've had to cut back on cooking with oil and thought I'd never be able to enjoy the taste of fried fish again. Thanks, Mr. Food, for coming up with this healthy option!"

Mexican Fish Tacos

Serves 6

- 1/2 cup sour cream
- 1/2 cup mayonnaise
- 1/4 cup chopped fresh cilantro
- 1 (1.25-ounce) package taco seasoning mix, divided
- 2 tablespoons vegetable oil
- 1 pound cod or other white-fleshed fish, cut into 1-inch pieces
- 1 (12-count) package taco shells, warmed
- 2 cups shredded lettuce
- 2 tomatoes, chopped

1. In a small bowl, combine sour cream, mayonnaise, cilantro, and 2 tablespoons taco seasoning; mix well and set aside for topping.

2. In a medium bowl, mix oil and remaining taco seasoning. Add fish and stir gently to coat.

3. Pour fish into a large skillet and cook over medium heat 4 to 5 minutes, or until it flakes easily.

4. Place fish in taco shells then top with lettuce, tomatoes, and sour cream topping.

SERVING TIP: I love serving this at parties! I fill up margarita glasses with each of the toppings – it makes for a fun presentation, and everybody can pile whatever they want on their tacos.

Crab Cakes

Makes 8 patties

3/4 cup plain bread crumbs

1/2 cup mayonnaise

1 egg

2 scallions, thinly sliced

2 tablespoons lemon juice

1 tablespoon Dijon-style mustard

1 tablespoon chopped fresh parsley

1 tablespoon Worcestershire sauce

1 teaspoon Old Bay Seasoning

2 (6-1/2-ounce) cans lump crabmeat, drained and cleaned

2 tablespoons butter

1 In a medium bowl, combine all ingredients except crabmeat and butter; mix well. Fold in crabmeat, being careful not to break it up. Form into 8 equal-sized patties.

2 In a large skillet, melt butter over medium heat. Sauté patties 3 to 4 minutes per side, or until browned. Serve immediately as is or with tartar, cocktail, or mustard sauce (see below).

TV Tidbit: Joe's Stone Crab Restaurant in Miami Beach is an institution. My friends there shared their special sauce recipe with me a long time ago and, when I shared it (with their permission) on one of my earliest shows, letters poured in from fans who'd been dying to get their hands on it for years!

Joe's Mustard Sauce

Makes about 1 cup

1 tablespoon plus 1/2 teaspoon mustard powder

1 cup mayonnaise

2 teaspoons Worcestershire sauce

1 teaspoon steak sauce

2 tablespoons heavy cream

2 tablespoons milk

Pinch of salt

1 In a medium bowl, combine mustard powder and mayonnaise; beat 1 minute.

2 Add remaining ingredients and beat until mixture is well blended and creamy. Cover and chill until ready to serve.

Crispy Calamari

Serves 2 to 4

1 pound cleaned calamari (squid) (see Tip)

3/4 cup all-purpose flour

1/2 teaspoon salt

1/2 teaspoon black pepper

1 cup vegetable oil

Marinara sauce, warmed (optional)

TIMESAVING TIP:
The easiest way to make this popular favorite is to buy calamari that's already cleaned, so you're ready to go when you get it home!

1 Cut tube-like calamari bodies into 1/2-inch rings, leaving tentacles intact.

2 In a large resealable plastic storage bag, combine flour, salt, and pepper. Add calamari in small batches and toss until completely coated.

3 In a large deep skillet, heat oil over medium-high heat until hot but not smoking. Fry calamari in small batches for 4 to 6 minutes, or until golden. Drain on paper towels and serve immediately as is or with your favorite marinara sauce for dipping.

Shrimp Scampi

Serves 6 to 8

1 pound uncooked linguine

2 tablespoons olive oil

1 pound medium shrimp, peeled and deveined, with tails left on

12 garlic cloves, crushed

1 teaspoon salt

1/2 teaspoon black pepper

1/2 cup dry white wine

2 tablespoons chopped fresh parsley

1 Cook linguine according to package directions; drain and cover to keep warm.

2 Meanwhile, in a large skillet, heat oil over medium-high heat. Add shrimp, garlic, salt, and pepper, and sauté 2 to 3 minutes, until shrimp are cooked through and pink.

3 Reduce heat to low and add wine and parsley; simmer 1 to 2 minutes.

4 Toss shrimp with linguine and serve immediately.

HEALTHY HINT: Watching your carbs and prefer to pass on the pasta? This tastes super over a bed of mixed greens for a hearty salad that won't tip the scales!

Ten-Minute Scallops

Serves 4

1/4 cup (1/2 stick) butter, melted

1/4 cup Italian-flavored bread crumbs

2 tablespoons chopped fresh parsley

1 teaspoon dried oregano

1 teaspoon minced garlic

1 pound sea scallops

1/4 teaspoon black pepper

1 Preheat broiler. Coat a large rimmed baking sheet with nonstick cooking spray; set aside.

2 In a small bowl, combine butter, bread crumbs, parsley, oregano, and garlic; mix well. Sprinkle scallops with pepper and place on baking sheet.

3 Spoon bread crumb mixture evenly over scallops and broil 8 to 10 minutes, or until topping is golden and scallops are cooked through.

NOTE: Watch the scallops carefully because, in seconds, the broiler can take them from golden to brown to burned!

SERVING TIP: Try this with my two-ingredient Chipotle Sauce for restaurant-fancy taste without the fancy restaurant tab!

Chipotle Sauce

Makes 1 cup

1 cup mayonnaise

1 tablespoon chipotle peppers in adobo sauce

1 Place ingredients in a blender or food processor and blend until smooth. Refrigerate until ready to serve.

Perfect Pasta

Rigatoni Bolognese

Serves 6 to 8

1 pound ground beef

1 carrot, shredded

1 medium onion, chopped

1 garlic clove, minced

2 (15-ounce) cans
tomato sauce

1 beef bouillon cube

1 teaspoon sugar

1 teaspoon dried basil

1 teaspoon dried oregano

1/2 teaspoon Italian seasoning

1-1/2 pounds rigatoni pasta

1 In a large pot, brown beef over medium-high heat. Drain off excess liquid then add carrot, onion, and garlic. Cook 4 to 5 minutes, or until onion is tender, stirring occasionally.

2 Add remaining ingredients except pasta, cover, and reduce heat to low. Simmer 20 minutes, stirring occasionally.

3 Meanwhile, cook pasta according to package directions; drain and place in a large serving bowl.

4 Pour sauce over pasta, toss to coat completely, and serve immediately.

TV Tidbit: This classic Italian pasta dish was featured during my week-long series saluting the Winter Olympics a few years back. Since we couldn't film on location in Italy, kudos to my team for creating a set to fit the theme perfectly!

Bow Ties Florentine

Serves 4 to 6

1 pound bow tie pasta

1 (7-ounce) jar Alfredo sauce

2 (9-ounce) packages frozen creamed spinach, thawed

1/2 teaspoon black pepper

1/2 teaspoon ground nutmeg

1 Cook pasta according to package directions; drain and return to pot.

2 Add Alfredo sauce, spinach, pepper, and nutmeg; mix well. Cook over medium heat 4 to 5 minutes, or until heated through; stir frequently. Serve immediately.

DID YOU KNOW... "Florentine" is a French cooking term that refers to foods cooked in the style of Florence, Italy, and served over or made with spinach?

Homestyle Macaroni & Cheese

Serves 6 to 8

1 pound elbow macaroni

1/4 cup (1/2 stick) butter

2 tablespoons all-purpose flour

1 teaspoon salt

1/2 teaspoon black pepper

2 cups milk

4 cups (16 ounces) shredded sharp Cheddar cheese, divided

1 Preheat oven to 375°F. Coat a 9" x 13" baking dish with nonstick cooking spray.

2 Cook macaroni according to package directions; drain. Place half in bottom of baking dish.

3 In a medium saucepan, melt butter over medium heat. Add flour, salt, and pepper; stir to mix well. Gradually add milk; bring to a boil and cook until thickened, stirring constantly. Sprinkle 1-1/2 cups cheese over macaroni in baking dish and top with half the white sauce. Repeat layers once more then top with remaining 1 cup cheese.

4 Bake 35 to 40 minutes, or until heated through and top is golden. Serve immediately.

HEALTHY HINT: This is sure to create smiles when you pack it in your kids' lunch thermoses. If they have it along with a cup of low-fat milk, they'll be well on their way to getting their daily calcium requirements.

Cold Sesame Noodles

Serves 4 to 6

1 pound linguine *or* spaghetti

1 cup peanut butter

6 scallions, thinly sliced

2 tablespoons vegetable oil

2 tablespoons soy sauce

3 garlic cloves, minced

1-1/2 teaspoons white vinegar

2 tablespoons sesame oil

1/4 teaspoon ground red pepper

1 Cook pasta according to package directions; drain and set aside.

2 In a large bowl, combine remaining ingredients; mix well. Add pasta and toss to coat evenly.

3 Cover and chill for at least 1 hour before serving (see Tip).

SERVING TIP: Sure, you can serve this warm but, to bring out the sesame and peanut flavors, I suggest serving it cold, which is the traditional way. And to give it a finished restaurant look, garnish with black and white sesame seeds and additional sliced scallions.

Roasted Red Pepper Ravioli

Serves 3 to 4

1 (24-ounce) package frozen cheese ravioli

1 (12-ounce) jar roasted red peppers, drained (see Option)

1 cup grated Parmesan cheese

1/2 cup half-and-half

2 garlic cloves

1 In a large pot, cook ravioli according to package directions; drain.

2 Meanwhile, in a food processor or blender, process peppers, Parmesan cheese, half-and-half, and garlic until smooth.

3 Add red pepper sauce to ravioli; toss gently until well coated. Serve immediately.

OPTION: Instead of jarred roasted peppers, you can roast your own in the oven or on the grill with a drizzle of heart-healthy olive oil. The garden-fresh taste is worth the few extra minutes of cooking!

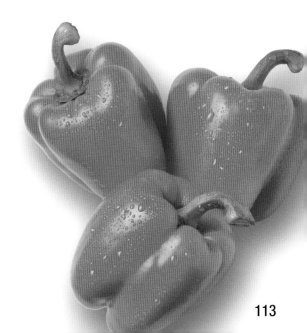

Spaghetti Pie

Serves 6

1/2 pound cooked spaghetti

2 tablespoons olive oil *or* melted butter

2 large eggs, well beaten

1/2 cup plus 2 tablespoons grated Parmesan cheese, divided

1 cup ricotta cheese

1 cup spaghetti sauce

1/2 cup (2 ounces) shredded mozzarella cheese

1 Preheat oven to 350°F.

2 In a large bowl, toss spaghetti with olive oil.

3 In a small bowl, combine eggs and 1/2 cup Parmesan cheese. Stir into spaghetti then pour into a lightly greased 10-inch pie plate, and form into a "crust."

4 Spread ricotta evenly over crust, but not quite to edge, and top with spaghetti sauce.

5 Bake uncovered for 25 minutes then top with shredded mozzarella and bake 5 more minutes, or until cheese melts.

6 Remove from oven and sprinkle with remaining 2 tablespoons Parmesan cheese. Cool 10 minutes before slicing into wedges.

TIMESAVING TIP: This family-friendly spaghetti dish works well made in advance and frozen without cooking. Thaw then bake just before serving.

114

Tomato Brie Pasta

Serves 4 to 6

1 pound linguine

1/2 cup olive oil

8 ounces brie cheese (with rind), cut into 1/2-inch cubes

3 large ripe tomatoes, chopped

1 cup fresh basil leaves, thinly sliced

3 garlic cloves, minced

1/2 teaspoon salt

1/4 teaspoon black pepper

1/3 cup grated Parmesan cheese

1 Cook linguine according to package directions; drain.

2 Meanwhile, in a large bowl, combine oil, brie, tomatoes, basil, garlic, salt, and pepper; mix well.

3 Add pasta and toss until well combined. Sprinkle with the Parmesan cheese and serve warm.

TV Tidbit: My team always (well, almost always!) enjoys tasting the recipes we share on my shows, but this one is especially memorable because of the novel addition of the brie. We have a lot of cheese fanatics here who were counting the minutes until the cameras stopped rolling so they could dig in!

Better Baked Ziti

Serves 6 to 8

1/2 pound ziti

1 (15-ounce) container ricotta cheese

3 cups (12 ounces) shredded mozzarella cheese, divided

3 cups spaghetti sauce, divided

1/2 cup grated Parmesan cheese

1 Preheat oven to 350°F. Coat a 9" x 13" baking pan with nonstick baking spray.

2 In a large pot of boiling, salted water, cook ziti until just barely tender; drain and place in a large bowl. Mix ricotta cheese and half the mozzarella cheese with ziti.

3 Cover bottom of pan with half the spaghetti sauce. Spoon ziti mixture into pan; cover with remaining spaghetti sauce. Sprinkle with Parmesan cheese and top with remaining mozzarella cheese.

4 Bake 20 to 30 minutes, or until cheese melts and is light golden.

HEALTHY HINT: Make this one a bit healthier by using whole-grain pasta and lighter versions of the ricotta and mozzarella cheese. Regular or light…either way, it'll be a huge hit!

Tuna Twist

Serves 6 to 8

1/2 pound twist pasta

2 cups mayonnaise

1/4 cup apple cider vinegar

1/4 teaspoon black pepper

1 (12-ounce) can tuna, drained and flaked

1 (10-ounce) package frozen peas, thawed

2 ribs celery, thinly sliced

1/2 small red onion, chopped

1/4 cup snipped fresh dill *or* 1 tablespoon dried dill weed

1 Cook pasta according to package directions; drain, rinse, and drain again.

2 In a large bowl, combine mayonnaise, vinegar, and pepper; mix well. Add pasta and remaining ingredients. Toss till well combined.

3 Cover salad and chill at least 2 hours before serving.

TIMESAVING TIP: This is a great make-ahead recipe. If you prepare it a day before you need it, not only is it ready when you are, but it's more flavorful, since the flavors get a chance to "marry" in the fridge overnight! Stir in some extra mayonnaise before serving if it needs more moisture.

Italian Sunday Dinner

Serves 4 to 6

- 1 pound ground beef
- 3/4 cup plain dry bread crumbs
- 1/2 cup grated Parmesan cheese
- 1/2 cup water
- 1/4 cup coarsely chopped fresh parsley
- 1 egg
- 1-1/2 teaspoons garlic powder
- 1 teaspoon salt
- 1 teaspoon black pepper
- 1 (26-1/2-ounce) jar spaghetti sauce
- 1 (28-ounce) can crushed tomatoes
- 1 teaspoon dried oregano
- 1 pound spaghetti

1 In a large bowl, combine ground beef, bread crumbs, Parmesan cheese, water, parsley, egg, garlic powder, salt, and black pepper; mix well. Form mixture into 12 meatballs then brown meatballs in a large pot over medium-high heat.

2 Add spaghetti sauce, crushed tomatoes, and oregano; reduce heat to medium low, and simmer 30 minutes, or until no pink remains in meatballs.

3 Meanwhile, cook the spaghetti according to package directions; drain.

4 Serve meatballs and sauce over spaghetti.

DID YOU KNOW...
many Italian Americans refer to tomato-based sauces as "gravy"? In many Italian households, gravy is long-cooked on Sunday mornings for serving up hot and hearty at traditional afternoon family dinners.

Lasagna Roll-Ups

Serves 4 to 6

1 (26-1/2-ounce) jar spaghetti sauce, divided

1 (2-pound) container ricotta cheese

2 (8-ounce) cups mozzarella cheese, divided

1/3 cup grated Parmesan cheese

3 eggs

1 tablespoon fresh chopped parsley

1 teaspoon salt

12 to 14 lasagna noodles, prepared according to package directions

1 Preheat oven to 375°F. Pour half the spaghetti sauce over the bottom of a 9" x 13" baking dish.

2 In a medium bowl, combine the ricotta cheese, 1 cup mozzarella cheese, the Parmesan cheese, eggs, parsley, and salt until well blended.

3 Spoon cheese mixture over lasagna noodles, distributing evenly, and roll up tightly. Place roll-ups seam-side down in baking dish; top with remaining sauce. Sprinkle with remaining mozzarella cheese.

4 Bake 35 to 40 minutes, or until heated through.

SERVING TIP: The nice part about these is how easy they are to portion. Everybody gets his or her very own roll-up (or two!)

Stuffed Shells

Serves 6 to 8

1 (12-ounce) package jumbo pasta shells

1 (32-ounce) container ricotta cheese

3 cups (12 ounces) shredded mozzarella cheese, divided

1/2 cup plus 2 tablespoons grated Parmesan cheese, divided

2 eggs

1 tablespoon chopped fresh parsley

3 garlic cloves, minced

1/2 teaspoon salt

1/2 teaspoon black pepper

1 (26-1/2-ounce) jar spaghetti sauce

1 Preheat oven to 350°F. Coat a 9" x 13" baking dish with nonstick cooking spray. Cook shells according to package directions; drain.

2 Meanwhile, in a large bowl, combine ricotta cheese, 2 cups mozzarella cheese, 1/2 cup Parmesan cheese, the eggs, parsley, garlic, salt, and pepper; mix well.

3 Spread 1 cup spaghetti sauce evenly over bottom of baking dish. Spoon ricotta mixture into a pastry tube or large resealable plastic storage bag with a corner snipped off. Squeeze about 1 tablespoon cheese mixture into each shell; place filled shells in baking dish and pour remaining spaghetti sauce over filled shells.

4 Cover shells with aluminum foil, and bake 40 minutes.

5 Remove foil, and sprinkle remaining 1 cup mozzarella cheese and 2 tablespoons Parmesan cheese over shells. Bake 10 to 12 more minutes, or until shells are heated through and cheese is golden and bubbling. Let sit 10 minutes before serving.

DID YOU KNOW...
the Italian name for shell-shaped pasta, *conchiglia*, translates to "conch"? These jumbo shells do resemble conch shells, don't they?

Rich 'n' Creamy Fettuccine

Serves 4 to 6

1 pound fettuccine (see Options)

1/2 cup (1 stick) butter

2 cups (1 pint) heavy cream

1/2 teaspoon black pepper

1 cup grated Parmesan cheese

1 Cook fettuccine according to package directions; drain.

2 Meanwhile, in a medium skillet, melt butter over medium-low heat and stir in cream and pepper. Cook 6 to 8 minutes, or until hot, stirring constantly.

3 Stir in Parmesan cheese; mix well and cook 3 to 5 minutes, or until thickened. Toss with fettuccine and serve immediately.

OPTIONS: I like to use spinach fettuccine to give this nice color contrast. And go ahead and top it with additional Parmesan cheese, if you'd like.

SERVING TIP: Have an Italian night in by setting your table with a red-and-white checkered tablecloth. Serve this up with a bottle of red wine, some crispy breadsticks, and an easy bagged Caesar salad. Then, as they say in Italy, *Mangia!* (Eat!)

Pesto Linguine

Serves 4 to 6

1 pound linguine

2 cups lightly packed
  fresh basil leaves

1 cup olive oil

1 cup grated Parmesan
  cheese

2 garlic cloves

1/2 cup pine nuts or walnuts

1/2 teaspoon salt

1 tablespoon lemon juice

1 In a soup pot, cook linguine according to package directions; drain and return to pot.

2 Meanwhile, in a blender or food processor, make pesto sauce by combining remaining ingredients; blend until smooth.

3 Add pesto sauce to drained linguine, toss until well combined, and serve.

SERVING TIP: Serve this topped with freshly grated Parmesan cheese and a few toasted pine nuts.

Upside-Down Noodle Wreath

Serves 12 to 14

1/2 cup packed light brown sugar

16 maraschino cherries

1/4 cup (1/2 stick) butter, melted

6 eggs

1 cup sour cream

3/4 cup granulated sugar

1 teaspoon vanilla extract

1/2 teaspoon salt

1 (20-ounce) can crushed pineapple, well drained

1 (16-ounce) package fine egg noodles, cooked and drained

1 Preheat oven to 350°F. Coat a 10-inch Bundt pan with nonstick cooking spray.

2 Sprinkle brown sugar into bottom of pan and place cherries evenly over brown sugar. Pour melted butter evenly over brown sugar and cherries; set aside.

3 In a large bowl, beat eggs, sour cream, granulated sugar, vanilla, and salt until well blended. Stir in crushed pineapple then drained noodles.

4 Pour evenly into Bundt pan and bake 70 minutes, or until center is set and top is golden. Allow to cool 20 minutes then invert gently onto a serving platter (see Tip).

SERVING TIP: Run a knife around the edges of the pan to help loosen the noodle wreath. And be careful when inverting it onto a platter, because it will be very hot!

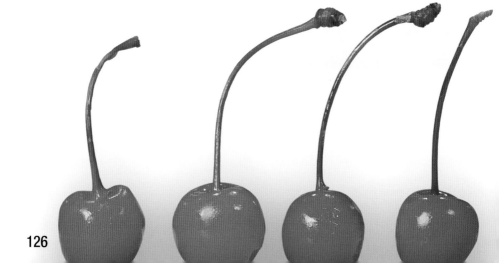

Sensational Sides

Double-Stuffed Potatoes

Serves 6

6 medium potatoes

1/4 cup sour cream

3 tablespoons butter

1/4 teaspoon onion powder

1/2 teaspoon salt

1/4 teaspoon black pepper

Paprika for sprinkling

1 Preheat oven to 400°F. Scrub potatoes then pierce each several times with a fork.

2 Bake 55 minutes, or until tender; let cool slightly.

3 Slice about 1/2 inch off top of each potato and scoop out pulp, leaving about a 1/4-inch-thick potato shell.

4 Place pulp in a medium bowl. Add sour cream, butter, onion powder, salt, and black pepper and beat with an electric beater. Spoon mixture into potato shells and sprinkle lightly with paprika.

5 Bake 30 minutes, or until potatoes begin to brown on top.

TV Tidbit: I feel really privileged to have so many opportunities for extraordinary food experiences. One was seeing just how Idaho potatoes get from the fields to our produce counters. Of course, after that, I was so inspired that I made this doubly good recipe with my Idaho potatoes. You're gonna love 'em!

Potato Puffs

Makes 24 large or 72 small puffs

3 pounds potatoes, peeled and quartered

1 large onion, chopped (see Tip)

3 tablespoons olive oil

1 cup cracker crumbs

2 teaspoons salt

1/2 teaspoon black pepper

2 egg yolks, beaten

1 Preheat oven to 400°F.

2 Place potatoes in a soup pot and add just enough water to cover them. Bring to a boil over high heat then reduce heat to medium and cook 12 to 15 minutes, or until fork-tender. Drain off water, mash potatoes, and allow to cool.

3 Coat a baking sheet with nonstick cooking spray.

4 In a small saucepan, sauté onion in olive oil over medium heat until tender. Add to mashed potatoes with cracker crumbs, salt, and pepper; mash mixture then, with your hands, roll mixture into balls and place potato balls on baking sheet.

5 Brush potato balls with egg yolk and bake 40 to 45 minutes, or until golden and crusty.

TIMESAVING TIP: Always in a rush? If you keep chopped onion in an airtight container in the freezer, it can be a real timesaver for recipes like this one.

Homestyle Potato Salad

Serves 12

4 pounds white *or* red potatoes

10 hard-boiled eggs, peeled and chopped

1/2 green or red bell pepper, diced

3 ribs celery, chopped

1 cup sour cream

1 cup mayonnaise

1 tablespoon white vinegar

2 tablespoons milk

1 tablespoon sugar

1 teaspoon salt

1/2 teaspoon black pepper

1 Place potatoes in a large soup pot, cover with water, and bring to a boil over high heat. Cook 25 to 30 minutes, or until fork-tender. Drain and cool slightly.

2 Cut potatoes into chunks and place in a large bowl. Add egg, bell pepper, and celery; set aside.

3 In a medium bowl, combine remaining ingredients; mix well. Pour sour cream mixture over potatoes and mix until thoroughly combined. Chill 2 to 3 hours before serving.

HEALTHY HINT: To make a lower-fat version of this traditional party favorite, substitute reduced-fat sour cream, light mayonnaise, and nonfat milk.

TV Tidbit: We taped the show for this picnic favorite at a local park. There happened to be a group of seniors nearby, enjoying a lively game of bingo, with the caller using a megaphone. My microphone was picking up all their sound, so my producer asked if they could turn it down. When they found out what we were doing, they ditched the game and became my spontaneous audience!

Sweet 'n' Sour Coleslaw

Serves 6 to 8

1/4 cup (1/2 stick) butter

1/2 cup cider vinegar

1/2 cup sugar

2 tablespoons all-purpose flour

1 teaspoon dry mustard

1/4 teaspoon garlic powder

1 teaspoon salt

1/2 teaspoon black pepper

1 egg, lightly beaten

2 (16-ounce) packages coleslaw mix (see Option)

1 In a medium saucepan, melt butter over medium heat. Add vinegar, sugar, flour, mustard, garlic powder, salt, and pepper; whisk until well combined.

2 Slowly whisk in the egg. Cook 1 to 2 minutes, or until mixture thickens, whisking constantly. Remove from heat and allow to cool slightly.

3 In a large bowl, combine coleslaw mix and vinegar mixture; toss until well coated. Serve, or cover and chill until ready to serve.

OPTION: This can also be made using whole cabbage. Just shred a medium-sized head of green cabbage and half a head of red cabbage. I also add some shredded carrot for color.

DID YOU KNOW...carrots weren't always orange? Native to Afghanistan, the earliest carrots were actually purple, red, black then pale yellow. In the seventeenth century, the Dutch developed the first orange carrots, which eventually were brought to the New World.

Sweet Potato Pancakes

Serves 8

1-1/2 pounds sweet potatoes, peeled and shredded

1 small onion, finely chopped

1 egg, beaten

1/2 cup all-purpose flour

1 teaspoon baking powder

1 teaspoon salt

1/2 teaspoon black pepper

Vegetable oil for frying

1 Place potatoes and onion in a fine strainer. Press down on mixture with the back of a large spoon to extract excess moisture. (If still watery, wrap them in a clean, old dishtowel and squeeze firmly.)

2 In a large bowl, combine potatoes and onion, egg, flour, baking powder, salt, and pepper; mix well. Form into 8 equal-sized pancakes.

3 In a large deep skillet, heat about 1/4 inch oil over medium-high heat. Place 4 pancakes in oil, without crowding skillet. Fry pancakes 2 to 3 minutes per side, or until golden. Continue with remaining pancakes. (If you like them crisper, fry until they're flecked with brown.) Drain on a paper towel-lined platter and serve warm.

SERVING TIP: For an extra-special treat, serve these topped with a drizzle of maple syrup to add a sweet touch, or a spoonful of cranberry relish to add a zesty tang!

133

Sweet Potato Casserole

Serves 6 to 8

1 cup chopped pecans

1 cup packed light brown sugar

1/3 cup all-purpose flour

1/2 cup (1 stick) butter, softened, divided

1/4 cup sweetened flaked coconut (optional)

2 (29-ounce) cans sweet potatoes, drained and mashed (see Tip)

3/4 cup granulated sugar

2 eggs

1/2 cup milk

1 teaspoon vanilla extract

1/2 teaspoon salt

1 Preheat oven to 350°F. Coat a 3-quart casserole dish with nonstick cooking spray.

2 In a medium bowl, combine pecans, brown sugar, flour, 1/4 cup butter, and the coconut, if desired; mix until crumbly then set aside.

3 In a large bowl, combine remaining ingredients, including remaining 1/4 cup butter; mix well. Spoon into casserole dish and sprinkle evenly with pecan mixture.

4 Bake 45 to 50 minutes, or until bubbly and heated through.

TV Tidbit: Here's one of my funniest stories! When we were taking photos of this recipe, we had a new kitchen assistant helping out. He didn't speak much English and, when he overheard my director and producer say, "We'll shoot Mr. Food tomorrow morning," he thought they were plotting my demise! When it was all cleared up, we all had a big laugh!

134

Spaghetti Rice

Serves 5 to 6

4 tablespoons vegetable oil, divided

1 (4-ounce) can mushroom slices *or* mushroom stems and pieces, drained

1 cup chopped onion (about 1 medium-sized onion)

1 cup (about 4 ounces) spaghetti, broken into 3-inch pieces

1-1/2 cups long-grain or whole-grain rice, uncooked

3-1/2 cups chicken broth

1/4 teaspoon salt

1/8 teaspoon pepper

1 In a large saucepan, heat 3 tablespoons oil over medium-high heat; add mushrooms and onions, and sauté until light brown. Remove from pan and set aside.

2 Heat remaining oil in saucepan and brown spaghetti over medium-low heat. (Be careful – it browns quickly.) Remove pan from heat.

3 Return mushrooms and onions to pan. Add remaining ingredients, mixing well. Bring mixture to a boil, reduce heat to low, cover, and cook 20 more minutes, or until all liquid is absorbed.

TIMESAVING TIP: Not only does this dish satisfy everyone – whether they want rice or pasta, but if you're looking for a good make-ahead dish, it freezes and reheats well for a winning side dish that can be ready in no time.

Mushroom Charlotte

Serves 8 to 10

1 pound orzo pasta, cooked and drained

1/4 cup (1/2 stick) butter or margarine, melted

1 (4-ounce) can sliced mushrooms *or* mushroom stems and pieces, drained

1 envelope (from a 2-ounce box) onion soup mix

1 Preheat oven to 350°F.

2 Place pasta in a large bowl; stir in melted butter. Add mushrooms and onion soup mix; mix well. Place in a 1-1/2-quart casserole dish.

3 Bake 30 minutes, or until hot and bubbly. Serve immediately.

TV Tidbit: When I taped a new show recently featuring this classic recipe, I decided to fancy it up by putting it in a mold. When I went to remove it from the mold, which I usually do with no problems, it was like a comedy routine. The first one wouldn't come out, the second one flew all over the counter. My team scrambled in to clean up and bring replacements, but no matter what I did, it wouldn't work. We laughed until we cried…and when I finally got it right, everyone applauded!

Mushroom Trio

Serves 6

4 tablespoons (1/2 stick) butter

1 small red onion, thinly sliced

1/4 teaspoon black pepper

1 (8-ounce) package white mushrooms, sliced

1 (6-ounce) package Portobello mushrooms, sliced

1 (3.5-ounce) package shiitake mushrooms, sliced

2 tablespoons bourbon *or* dry red wine

2 tablespoons Worcestershire sauce

1/2 teaspoon salt

1 In a large skillet, melt butter over medium-high heat. Add onion and black pepper, and sauté 4 to 5 minutes, or until onion is tender.

2 Add mushrooms and sauté 5 to 7 minutes, or until softened.

3 Add remaining ingredients and bring to a boil. Cook 1 minute, or until sauce thickens.

SERVING TIP: Mushrooms pair well with everything, and this hearty trio is no exception! Try 'em topping steaks, chops, or even burgers for a burst of flavor!

Summer Squash Bake

Serves 12

4 pounds summer (yellow) squash, diced

1 medium onion, diced

1/2 cup water

1 (10-3/4-ounce) can condensed cream of mushroom soup

1 cup (4 ounces) shredded Cheddar cheese

1/2 teaspoon salt

3/4 teaspoon black pepper

2 cups cornflakes, coarsely crushed

1/4 cup (1/2 stick) butter, melted

1 Preheat oven to 350°F. Coat a 9" x 13" baking dish with nonstick cooking spray.

2 In a large saucepan, cook squash and onion in water over medium heat 15 minutes, or until tender; drain well.

3 In a medium bowl, combine drained squash mixture, the soup, cheese, salt, and pepper; mix well and pour into baking dish. Sprinkle with crushed cornflakes and drizzle with melted butter.

4 Bake 18 to 20 minutes, or until heated through and topping is golden.

DID YOU KNOW...even though summer squash is yellow in color, it is very eco-friendly – a real "green" veggie? You see, as opposed to the many varieties of winter squash, every bit of summer squash is edible...the rind, seeds, and all!

Zucchini Squares

Serves 6 to 8

4 eggs

1/2 cup grated Parmesan cheese

1/2 cup chopped onion

1/2 teaspoon seasoned salt

1/2 teaspoon dried oregano

1/2 teaspoon garlic powder

1/4 cup chopped fresh parsley *or* 2 tablespoons dried parsley flakes (optional)

1/2 cup vegetable oil

1/2 cup all-purpose flour

1 cup biscuit baking mix

3 cups grated zucchini

1 Preheat oven to 375°F. In a large bowl, beat eggs; add remaining ingredients and mix well. Pour mixture into an ungreased 9-inch square broiler-proof baking dish.

2 Bake 30 to 35 minutes, until set and cooked through.

3 To brown the top, place pan under a preheated broiler for the last 2 or 3 minutes of cooking. Cool for 3 to 5 minutes then cut into squares and serve.

VIEWER FEEDBACK: I got a letter from a young woman who told me she was disappointed after making this recipe for her new husband – she said it didn't look or taste good. Fortunately, Patty, my test kitchen director, figured out she was using cucumbers instead of zucchini! The woman wrote back to tell me how embarrassed she was by her mistake, and that her zucchini version was a big hit! Now she sometimes even makes it with summer squash.

Saucy Brussels Sprouts

Serves 4 to 6

2 (10-ounce) packages
frozen Brussels sprouts
(see Option)

1/4 cup (1/2 stick) butter

1 (7/8-ounce) package
béarnaise sauce mix

1 cup milk

1 teaspoon yellow mustard

1 Cook Brussels sprouts according to package directions; drain.

2 Melt butter in a medium skillet over medium heat. Add the béarnaise sauce mix; mix well. Add milk and mustard and bring to a boil. Cook 1 minute, or until thickened, stirring constantly.

3 Add Brussels sprouts and stir until well coated and heated through. Serve immediately.

OPTION: If you'd rather use fresh Brussels sprouts, trim the stems and peel off the tough outer leaves, if necessary. Then carefully make an "X" with a knife in the bottom of each and cook until tender before proceeding with step 2.

Vegetable Stir-Fry

Serves 8

1 (15-ounce) can baby corn, drained and liquid reserved

2 tablespoons light soy sauce

2 tablespoons cornstarch

1 teaspoon crushed red pepper

1/4 cup peanut oil

4 garlic cloves, minced

1 bunch broccoli, cut into small florets

2 medium bell peppers (1 red and 1 yellow), cut into 1/2-inch strips

1 large onion, cut into wedges

1/2 pound fresh sliced mushrooms

1/2 pound snow peas, trimmed

1 In a small bowl, combine reserved liquid from the corn, the soy sauce, cornstarch, and crushed red pepper; set aside.

2 In a large skillet or wok, heat peanut oil over high heat until hot. Add garlic, broccoli, peppers, onions, and mushrooms. Stir-fry 6 to 7 minutes, or until vegetables are crisp-tender.

3 Add snow peas and baby corn, and stir-fry 3 to 4 minutes, or until snow peas turn bright green.

4 Add soy sauce mixture, and stir-fry 1 to 2 minutes, or until sauce thickens. Serve immediately.

HEALTHY HINT: For ages, moms have told their kids, "Eat your vegetables – they're good for you!" Well, current research shows that broccoli and other green vegetables included in a low-fat diet help our vision, strengthen our bones and teeth, and can also contribute to lowering our risk of certain cancers. Wow! This should convince all of us to eat our veggies!

Stuffed Artichokes

Serves 4

4 large artichokes, trimmed

1/4 teaspoon salt

1/4 cup olive oil, divided

4 tablespoons (1/2 stick) butter

1 medium-sized onion, chopped

2 teaspoons minced garlic

1 cup Italian-flavored bread crumbs

1 teaspoon grated Parmesan cheese

1 Place artichokes and salt in a large pot and fill pot with just enough water to cover artichokes. Bring to a boil over high heat and cook 35 to 40 minutes, or until artichokes are tender.

2 Remove artichokes and allow to drain upside-down; place in an 8-inch square baking dish and set aside.

3 Preheat oven to 375°F.

4 In a medium skillet, heat 3 tablespoons oil and the butter over medium heat; add the onion and garlic. Cook 3 minutes, or until onion is tender. Remove skillet from heat and stir in bread crumbs and Parmesan cheese.

5 Spread artichoke leaves apart and fill spaces between leaves with stuffing mixture. Drizzle remaining 1 tablespoon olive oil over artichokes. Cover tightly with aluminum foil and bake 15 to 20 minutes, or until hot. Serve immediately.

Classic Creamed Spinach

Serves 4 to 6

2 tablespoons butter

2 tablespoons all-purpose flour

2 (10-ounce) packages frozen chopped spinach, thawed and well drained (see Option)

1 cup (1/2 pint) heavy cream

1/2 teaspoon ground nutmeg

1/2 teaspoon garlic powder

1/2 teaspoon salt

1 In a large skillet, melt butter over medium heat; stir in flour until mixture is combined and golden.

2 Add remaining ingredients; mix well and cook 3 to 5 minutes, or until heated through.

OPTION: Two 10-ounce packages of fresh spinach can also be used; just chop it and boil until tender then drain well and proceed as directed.

Sautéed Green Beans

Serves 8

2 tablespoons olive oil

1/4 cup slivered almonds

1 garlic clove, minced

2 (9-ounce) packages frozen French-cut green beans

1/4 cup sun-dried tomatoes, chopped

1/4 teaspoon salt

1/4 teaspoon black pepper

1 In a large skillet, heat oil over medium heat. Add almonds and garlic, and sauté 2 to 3 minutes, or until almonds are light golden.

2 Add remaining ingredients, cover, and allow beans to steam 10 minutes, or until tender, stirring occasionally. Serve immediately.

Carrot Bake

Serves 6 to 8

3 (4-ounce) jars carrot baby food

1/2 cup (1 stick) butter, melted

3 eggs

1 cup all-purpose flour

1 cup packed light brown sugar

1 tablespoon lemon juice

1 teaspoon vanilla extract

1 teaspoon baking soda

1 teaspoon baking powder

1 Preheat oven to 350°F. Coat an 8-inch square baking dish with nonstick cooking spray.

2 In a large bowl, combine carrots and butter; mix well. Add remaining ingredients and mix until well blended; pour into baking dish.

3 Bake 35 to 40 minutes, or until a wooden toothpick inserted in center comes out clean.

OPTIONS: For a change of pace, try variations of this recipe using baby-food squash, pumpkin or corn in place of the carrots.

Best Breads & Muffins

Lemon Poppy Seed Bread

Serves 10 to 12

1/4 cup (1/2 stick) butter, softened

1/4 cup applesauce

1 cup sugar

2 eggs

1-1/2 cups all-purpose flour

1 teaspoon baking powder

1/2 teaspoon salt

1/2 cup milk

1 tablespoon grated lemon rind

1 teaspoon poppy seeds

1 Preheat oven to 350°F. Coat a 9" x 5" loaf pan with nonstick cooking spray.

2 In a medium bowl, beat butter, applesauce, sugar, and eggs until smooth.

3 In another medium bowl, combine flour, baking powder, and salt. Add to applesauce mixture, beating until well combined. Stir in milk, lemon rind, and poppy seeds.

4 Pour batter into loaf pan and bake 45 to 50 minutes, or until a wooden toothpick inserted in center comes out clean. Allow to cool in pan.

SERVING TIP: To make this even more lemony delicious, make an easy glaze by stirring together 3 tablespoons lemon juice and 1/4 cup confectioners' sugar until smooth and creamy. Pour over loaf after removing it from the oven then allow loaf to cool in pan.

DID YOU KNOW...poppy seeds were popular in baking and as a spread as far back as the Middle Ages? They add a nutty flavor to this everybody-loves-it quick bread.

148

Spoon Bread

Serves 9 to 12

2 cups milk

1-1/2 cups water

1-1/2 cups cornmeal

2 tablespoons butter

1-1/2 teaspoons sugar

1-1/4 teaspoons salt

5 eggs

1 tablespoon baking powder

1 Preheat oven to 350°F. Coat an 8-inch square baking dish with nonstick cooking spray.

2 In a medium saucepan, combine milk and water; simmer over medium-low heat until hot, stirring occasionally.

3 Add cornmeal, butter, sugar, and salt; stir 1 to 2 minutes, until mixture is thickened. Remove from heat.

4 In a medium bowl, beat eggs and baking powder until very light and fluffy. Stir in cornmeal mixture; mix well then spoon into baking dish.

5 Bake 45 to 50 minutes, or until top is golden. Serve hot.

TV Tidbit: When I taped my half-hour holiday special, *Mr. Food: An Old-Fashioned Christmas*, we traveled to historic Colonial Williamsburg in Virginia, where the chef at Christiana Campbell's Tavern graciously shared this classic recipe with me…for you. All I can say is "Thanks" and "Yum, yum, yum!"

"Bapple" Bread

Serves 10 to 12

4 ripe bananas

1 cup sugar

1/2 cup applesauce

2 eggs

1 teaspoon baking soda

1 tablespoon baking powder

1 teaspoon salt

1 teaspoon vanilla extract

2 cups all-purpose flour

1 Preheat oven to 350°F. Coat a 9" x 5" loaf pan with nonstick cooking spray.

2 Place bananas in a large bowl and mash with an electric mixer. Stir in sugar and let stand 15 minutes.

3 Add applesauce and eggs, and beat well. Add remaining ingredients and mix thoroughly. Pour mixture into loaf pan.

4 Bake 55 minutes, or until a wooden toothpick inserted in center comes out clean. Remove from oven and let stand 10 minutes before removing from pan. Cool on a wire rack.

HEALTHY HINT: This "no oil required" quick bread is perfect for anyone watching what they eat. It tastes heavenly, and nobody will ever know we used applesauce in place of oil!

Fresh Tomato Flatbread

Serves 6

1 (8-ounce) package refrigerated crescent rolls

1 large tomato, thinly sliced

1/2 medium-sized onion, thinly sliced

2 tablespoons olive oil

1 teaspoon dried Italian seasoning

1 teaspoon chopped garlic

1/4 teaspoon salt

1/8 teaspoon black pepper

1 tablespoon grated Parmesan cheese

1 Preheat oven to 375°F. Coat a large rimmed baking sheet with nonstick cooking spray.

2 Unroll packaged dough and press seams together to form a complete crust. Place sliced tomato and onion over crust.

3 In a small bowl, combine remaining ingredients except Parmesan cheese; mix well then brush over sliced tomato, onion, and crust. Sprinkle with Parmesan cheese.

4 Bake 17 to 20 minutes, or until golden. Cut into squares, and serve.

SERVING TIP: Garnish with slivered fresh basil, if you'd like.

VIEWER FEEDBACK: "Dear Mr. Food, I'm the world's worst baker, and when I served this to company recently, everyone thought I took a baking class! I didn't tell them I made it with refrigerated dough! Thank you for making me look so good!" You're welcome, "Tanya from Illinois"! (And you can easily fill your bread basket with this fresh-tasting, great-looking treat, too!)

Yorkshire Pudding Popovers

Makes 6 popovers

2 cold eggs

1 cup cold milk

1 tablespoon butter, melted

1 cup all-purpose flour

2 scallions, thinly sliced

1/2 teaspoon garlic powder

1/2 teaspoon salt

1 Preheat oven to 425°F. Coat a 6-cup muffin tin with nonstick cooking spray.

2 In a large bowl, combine all ingredients and beat with a wooden spoon until smooth. Immediately pour batter into muffin cups, distributing evenly.

3 Bake 30 to 35 minutes, or until golden and puffy (see Note). Cool slightly before removing from muffin cups. Serve immediately.

NOTE: These will "pop" up better if you don't open the oven until nearly the end of the suggested cooking time.

SERVING TIP: Serve these as is, or with roasts for dipping in pan drippings. They give any meal an elegant touch.

Sweet Potato Biscuits

Makes 1 dozen

1 cup mashed canned sweet potatoes

1 cup milk

1/2 cup sugar

1 egg, beaten

1 tablespoon butter, melted

3 cups self-rising flour

1 teaspoon baking powder

1/2 teaspoon salt

1/2 cup vegetable shortening

1 Preheat oven to 400°F.

2 In a medium bowl, using a fork, mix sweet potatoes, milk, sugar, egg, and butter until well combined.

3 In a large bowl, combine flour, baking powder, and salt. Using 2 knives or a pastry cutter, cut shortening into flour mixture. Pour sweet potato mixture into flour mixture and mix until just combined. Drop mixture by large spoonfuls onto rimmed baking sheets.

4 Bake 15 to 17 minutes, or until golden. Serve warm.

SERVING TIP: At our house, we like to team these with a warm mixture of real maple syrup and a drop of melted butter for dipping. They sure are a treat!

Parsley Garlic Rolls

Makes 1 dozen

3 tablespoons butter, melted

2 tablespoons chopped
fresh parsley

2 garlic cloves, minced

1/2 teaspoon salt

1 (16-ounce) loaf frozen
bread dough, thawed

1 Coat a 12-cup muffin pan with nonstick cooking spray.

2 In a small bowl, combine melted butter, parsley, garlic, and salt; mix well.

3 On a lightly floured surface, roll bread dough into a 12-inch square. Spread parsley mixture over dough, leaving a 1/2-inch border on top and bottom edges. Roll dough tightly jellyroll fashion, starting at bottom edge. Pinch to seal edge.

4 Cut roll of dough into 1-inch-wide slices. Place each slice flat-side down in a cup of the muffin pan.

5 Cover and let rise in a warm place for 1 hour, or until doubled in size.

6 Preheat oven to 400°F. Bake rolls 9 to 11 minutes, or until golden. Remove from pan and serve warm.

TIMESAVING TIP:
These reheat well, so if you're having company and want to make them ahead to leave room in your oven for other items, just keep 'em in an airtight container and reheat for about 5 minutes before serving.

Cheesecake French Toast

Serves 4

1 (3-ounce) package cream cheese, softened

2 tablespoons confectioners' sugar

2 tablespoons strawberry preserves

8 slices country white bread

2 eggs

1/2 cup half-and-half

2 tablespoons granulated sugar

4 tablespoons (1/2 stick) butter

1 In a small bowl, combine cream cheese and confectioners' sugar; mix well then stir in preserves. Spread equally over 4 bread slices. Top with remaining bread slices, forming sandwiches.

2 In a shallow bowl, whisk eggs, half-and-half, and granulated sugar until well combined.

3 In a large skillet, melt 2 tablespoons butter over medium heat. Dip each sandwich into egg mixture, completely coating both sides. Cook 2 sandwiches at a time for 1 to 2 minutes per side, or until golden. Melt remaining 2 tablespoons butter in skillet and cook remaining 2 sandwiches. Slice each in half diagonally and serve.

SERVING TIP: Make this look and taste extra-fancy by topping it with additional confectioners' sugar or maple syrup and/or fresh fruit. It sure makes you want to eat breakfast more often, doesn't it?

Blueberry Muffins

Makes 1 dozen

1-1/4 cups plus 2 tablespoons sugar, divided

1/2 cup (1 stick) butter, softened

2 eggs

2 cups all-purpose flour

2 teaspoons baking powder

1/2 teaspoon salt

1/2 cup milk

1 teaspoon vanilla extract

1 (12-ounce) package frozen *or* 1 pint fresh blueberries

1 Preheat oven to 375°F. Line 12 muffin cups with paper baking cups and coat with nonstick cooking spray.

2 In a large bowl, with an electric beater on medium speed, beat 1-1/4 cups sugar and the butter until creamy. Add eggs one at a time, beating well after each addition. Add flour, baking powder, and salt; beat well. Add milk and vanilla and beat until thoroughly combined.

3 Mash 1/2 cup blueberries and stir into batter. Stir in remaining whole blueberries then spoon into baking cups, distributing batter evenly. Sprinkle tops with remaining 2 tablespoons sugar.

4 Bake 25 to 30 minutes, or until a wooden toothpick inserted in center comes out clean. Remove to a wire rack to cool completely.

OPTION: One recipe = two great tastes! Use this recipe to make chocolate chip muffins by replacing the blueberries with 1 cup chocolate chips. Just add 'em in place of the whole blueberries.

Upside-Down Pineapple Muffins

Makes 2 dozen

2 (20-ounce) cans sliced pineapple, drained

1 (8-1/4-ounce) can sliced pineapple, drained

24 maraschino cherries

1/2 cup packed light brown sugar

1 (18.25-ounce) package white cake mix

1/4 cup canola oil

3 egg whites

1 (20-ounce) can crushed pineapple, drained, with juice reserved

NOTE: Make sure to invert the muffins while still warm so they'll easily pop out of the muffin cups.

1 Preheat oven to 350°F. Coat 24 muffin cups with nonstick cooking spray.

2 Place a pineapple ring in the bottom of each cup. Place a cherry in the center of each pineapple ring and sprinkle each with an equal amount of brown sugar; set aside.

3 In a large bowl, with an electric beater on medium speed, beat cake mix, oil, egg whites, and reserved pineapple juice until well combined.

4 Stir in crushed pineapple and divide mixture evenly among the muffin cups.

5 Bake 20 to 25 minutes, or until golden. Allow to cool 15 minutes then invert muffins onto a cookie sheet. Allow to cool, and serve, or cover until ready to serve.

Garlic Pita Crisps

Serves 12

6 (6-inch) pita breads

2 tablespoons garlic powder

1-1/2 teaspoons salt

Nonstick cooking spray

1 Preheat oven to 350°F.

2 Cut each pita into 8 equal-sized wedges. Separate each wedge into 2 pieces.

3 In a large resealable plastic storage bag, combine garlic powder and salt. Coat both sides of pita wedges lightly with nonstick cooking spray then place about 1/4 of the wedges in the plastic bag; shake to coat.

4 Place wedges in a single layer on a large rimmed baking sheet. Repeat with remaining wedges and additional baking sheets.

5 Bake 15 minutes, or until golden and crisp; allow to cool. Serve immediately, or store in an airtight container until ready to use.

SERVING TIP:
Although I must admit that I love to eat these by themselves, they go perfectly with dips, especially my Roasted Red Pepper Hummus (page 6).

Decadent Desserts

Death by Chocolate

Serves up to 24 (or 1 serious chocoholic)

1 (19- to 21-ounce) package brownie mix, batter prepared according to package directions

1/4 cup coffee-flavored liqueur (see Options)

2 (2.8-ounce) packages instant chocolate mousse, prepared according to package directions (see Options)

8 (1.4-ounce) chocolate-covered toffee candy bars (such as Skor® or Heath®), coarsely crushed

1 (12-ounce) container frozen whipped topping, thawed

1 Preheat oven and bake brownie batter in a 9" x 13" baking pan according to package directions; allow to cool completely.

2 Use a fork to prick holes in top of cooled brownies; drizzle with coffee liqueur.

3 Break up brownies into small pieces. Coarsely crush candy bars in a food processor or by gently tapping the wrapped bars with a hammer. Place half the brownies in bottom of a trifle dish or large glass serving bowl. Cover with half the mousse then one-third of the crushed candy and half the whipped topping. Repeat layers and top with the remaining crushed candy.

4 Cover and chill at least 2 hours before serving.

OPTIONS: Instead of coffee liqueur, you can use a mixture of 1 teaspoon sugar and 1/4 cup leftover black coffee, or leave out the coffee flavoring entirely. And instead of chocolate mousse, you can prepare two (4-serving) packages of instant chocolate pudding.

VIEWER FEEDBACK: You keep asking what my most-requested recipes are, and this is my most popular dessert recipe of all time! Call it sinful, call it decadent…it's a chocoholic's dream come true!

Blueberry Coffee Cake

Serves 12 to 15

1 cup (2 sticks) butter

1-1/2 cups sugar

3 eggs

3 cups all-purpose flour

2 teaspoons baking powder

1 teaspoon vanilla extract

1 (21-ounce) can blueberry pie filling

Topping:

1/4 cup all-purpose flour

1/4 cup sugar

2 teaspoons butter

1 teaspoon ground cinnamon

1 Preheat oven to 350°F. Coat a 9" x 13" metal baking pan (see Note) with nonstick baking spray.

2 In a large bowl, cream 1 cup butter and 1-1/2 cups sugar. Add eggs one at a time. Add 3 cups flour, the baking powder, and vanilla; mix well.

3 Spread half the batter into baking pan. Using a wet knife, spread pie filling evenly over batter and cover evenly with remaining batter.

4 In a small bowl, mix together topping ingredients with a fork until crumbly then sprinkle over batter.

5 Bake 55 to 60 minutes, or until a wooden toothpick inserted in center comes out clean. Cool in pan on wire rack. Cut and serve.

NOTE: If you use a glass baking dish, this will cook a bit faster, so adjust your cooking time.

TV Tidbit: Every so often, a recipe from a viewer becomes a huge hit on my show. This is one that a fan gave me on a book tour a few years ago. I owe her a big THANK YOU!

Flourless Chocolate Cake

Serves 12 to 16

2 cups (12 ounces) semisweet chocolate chips

1/2 cup (1 stick) butter plus extra for coating

1/4 cup sugar

1/4 cup water

1 teaspoon instant coffee granules

3 eggs

1 Preheat oven to 425°F. Butter bottom and sides of a 9-inch pie plate. Place a 12-inch square sheet of wax paper in plate and butter the wax paper.

2 In a medium saucepan, combine chocolate chips, 1/2 cup butter, the sugar, water, and coffee granules; heat over medium heat 2 to 3 minutes, until chocolate and butter are melted, stirring constantly. Remove from heat and stir in the eggs one at a time, until mixture is smooth.

3 Pour mixture into wax paper-lined pie plate and bake 10 minutes. Cake will not be completely set in the middle. Cool, cover loosely, then chill 6 to 8 hours, or overnight.

4 When ready to serve, remove cake from refrigerator and allow to sit 10 minutes. Invert cake onto a large flat serving dish and remove wax paper. Top with dollops of whipped cream just before serving.

DID YOU KNOW...flourless cakes are perfect for people on a gluten-free diet, as well as for the holiday of Passover? No one ever misses it in this cake, 'cause it's so sinfully rich!

Million-Dollar Pound Cake

Serves 12 to 14

1 pound butter, softened

3 cups sugar

6 eggs

4 cups all-purpose flour

3/4 cup milk

1 teaspoon almond extract

1 teaspoon vanilla extract

Orange Glaze (below), optional

1 Preheat oven to 300°F. Grease and flour a 10-inch tube or Bundt pan.

2 In a large bowl, cream the butter; gradually add sugar, beating with an electric mixer on medium speed until light and fluffy.

3 Add eggs one at a time, beating after each addition. Gradually add flour alternately with milk, beginning and ending with flour and mixing well after each addition. Mix in almond and vanilla extracts.

4 Pour batter into pan and bake 1 hour and 40 minutes, or until a wooden toothpick inserted in center comes out clean. Cool in pan 10 to 15 minutes then remove to a wire rack. When completely cool, drizzle with Orange Glaze, if desired.

SERVING TIP: This is a nice, moist cake, so it's great served as is but it can also be topped with almost anything from fresh fruit to whipped cream to ice cream. Add your favorite toppings!

Orange Glaze
Makes about ½ cup

1-1/2 cups confectioners' sugar

2 tablespoons orange juice

1 In a small bowl, combine confectioners' sugar and orange juice with a wire whisk until smooth.

2 Drizzle over cooled cake, or almost any cool or room temperature cake or cookies.

Chocolate Chip Cheesecake

Serves 15 to 20

3 (8-ounce) packages cream
cheese, softened

3 eggs

3/4 cup sugar

1 teaspoon vanilla extract

2 (16.5-ounce) rolls
refrigerator chocolate
chip cookie dough

1 Preheat oven to 350°F.

2 In a large bowl, beat together cream cheese, eggs, sugar, and vanilla until well mixed; set aside.

3 Slice cookie dough rolls into 1/3-inch slices. Arrange slices from one roll over bottom of a greased 9" x 13" baking dish; press together until there are no holes in dough.

4 Spoon cream cheese mixture evenly over dough; top with remaining slices of cookie dough. (No need to press these together.)

5 Bake 45 to 50 minutes, or until golden and center is slightly firm. Remove from oven, let cool then refrigerate. Slice when well chilled.

SERVING TIP: Serve the cheesecake plain, with chocolate or fudge sauce, or whipped topping – whatever is your favorite.

Macadamia Cheesecake

Serves 12 to 14

1 (7-ounce) jar macadamia nuts, divided

1 cup plus 2 tablespoons sugar, divided

1 cup graham cracker crumbs

1/4 cup (1/2 stick) butter, melted

3 (8-ounce) packages cream cheese, softened

2 eggs

3/4 cup sour cream

2 (6-ounce) packages white baking bars, melted

1 Preheat oven to 350°F.

2 In a blender or food processor, finely chop 1/2 cup macadamia nuts with 2 tablespoons sugar. Place in a medium bowl and add graham cracker crumbs and melted butter; mix well then press into bottom of a 10-inch springform pan.

3 In a large bowl, with an electric beater on medium speed, beat cream cheese, the remaining 1 cup sugar, and the eggs until smooth. Add sour cream then the melted white baking bars, mixing until well combined after each addition.

4 With a knife, coarsely chop the remaining macadamia nuts and stir into cream cheese mixture; pour over crust.

5 Bake 45 to 50 minutes, until almost set in the center. Turn off oven and leave cheesecake in oven with door ajar for 1 hour. Remove from oven and allow to cool completely then cover and chill at least 4 hours, or overnight.

SERVING TIP: For even more pizzazz, garnish the top with some dark-chocolate-dipped macadamia nuts.

Mile-High Lemon Meringue Pie

Serves 8

1 folded, refrigerated pie crust (from a 15-ounce package)

1-1/2 cups sugar, divided

5 tablespoons cornstarch

1/4 teaspoon salt

1 cup water

1/2 cup milk

4 eggs, separated

1 tablespoon butter

1/2 cup fresh lemon juice

1/4 teaspoon cream of tartar

SERVING TIP: If you'd like, sprinkle each piece of pie with some grated fresh lemon peel just before serving. Talk about a double burst of sunshine!

1 Unfold pie crust and place in a 9-inch pie plate, pressing crust firmly into plate, then flute if desired. Bake pie shell according to package directions; let cool.

2 Meanwhile, in a medium saucepan, combine 1 cup sugar, the cornstarch, and salt; mix well. Gradually whisk in water and milk, stirring until cornstarch is dissolved. Cook over medium heat, whisking until mixture comes to a boil.

3 In a medium bowl, lightly beat the egg yolks. Gradually whisk in about 1/2 cup milk mixture then whisk yolk mixture back into saucepan. Simmer over low heat 2 to 3 minutes, whisking occasionally.

4 Remove pan from heat and whisk in butter and lemon juice. Pour into pie shell; set aside.

5 Preheat oven to 350°F. In a medium bowl, with an electric beater, beat egg whites with cream of tartar until soft peaks form. Add remaining 1/2 cup sugar and continue beating until stiff peaks form, making meringue.

6 Spread meringue over pie filling, sealing to edges of crust. Using a spatula or the back of a tablespoon, form peaks in meringue, and bake 12 to 15 minutes, or until meringue is golden. Let cool, then slice and serve.

Upside-Down Apple Pie

Serves 6 to 8

6 tablespoons (3/4 stick) butter, melted, divided

1/2 cup packed light brown sugar

1/2 cup chopped pecans

1 (15-ounce) package folded refrigerated pie crusts

1 cup granulated sugar

1/3 cup all-purpose flour

3/4 teaspoon ground cinnamon

5 large Granny Smith *or* other firm apples, peeled, cored, and cut into 1/2-inch wedges

PREPARATION TIP:
To make sure you don't have to do any oven cleanup, position a baking sheet on the bottom oven rack to catch any juices that may leak from the pie while it's baking.

1 Preheat oven to 375°F. Coat a deep-dish pie plate with nonstick cooking spray and line it with wax paper. Coat wax paper with nonstick cooking spray.

2 In a small bowl, combine 4 tablespoons butter, the brown sugar, and pecans; mix well and spread evenly over bottom of pie plate. Unfold 1 pie crust and place it in pie plate, pressing crust firmly against nut mixture and sides of plate; set aside.

3 In a large bowl, combine granulated sugar, flour, cinnamon, and remaining 2 tablespoons butter; mix well. Add apples and toss gently to coat. Spoon into pie crust.

4 Unfold second pie crust and place over apple mixture. Trim and fold edges together to seal. Using a knife, cut four 1-inch slits in top crust.

5 Bake 1 to 1-1/4 hours, or until crust is golden (see Tip). Carefully loosen wax paper around rim and invert pie onto a serving plate while still hot. Remove wax paper and allow to cool slightly. Slice and serve warm, or allow to cool completely before serving.

No-Roll Pie Crust

Makes 1 (9-inch) pie crust

1-1/2 cups all-purpose flour

2 tablespoons sugar

1/2 teaspoon salt

1/2 cup vegetable oil

2 tablespoons cold milk

1 In a 9-inch pie plate, combine flour, sugar, and salt. In a 1-cup measuring cup, whisk together oil and milk and pour over flour mixture.

2 Using a fork, mix until completely dampened. Press dough evenly over bottom of pan then up sides and over rim.

To use as an unbaked shell: Fill with desired pie filling and bake according to filling directions.

To use as a baked shell: Prick surface of dough with a fork several times and bake in a preheated 425°F. oven 12 to 15 minutes; cool and fill as desired.

OPTION: You can even use this crust for beef pot pies or with any other savory filling – just eliminate the 2 tablespoons sugar.

VIEWER FEEDBACK: Talk about feedback! This is a fan favorite that I have to make sure to share on TV every few years, since I always get requests for it. I'm glad you like it!

Two-Minute Hawaiian Pie

Serves 6 to 8

1 (20-ounce) can crushed pineapple in syrup, undrained

1 (6-serving-size) package instant vanilla pudding and pie filling (see note)

1 (8-ounce) container sour cream

1 (9-inch) prepared shortbread pie crust

1 (8-ounce) can sliced pineapple, drained and halved

8 maraschino cherries, drained

2 tablespoons sweetened flaked coconut

1 In a large bowl, combine crushed pineapple with its syrup, the dry pudding mix, and sour cream; mix until well combined. Spoon into pie crust and decorate the top with pineapple and cherries; sprinkle with coconut.

2 Cover and chill at least 2 hours before serving.

VIEWER FEEDBACK: Over the years, a few of you have written to ask about the pudding mix that goes in here, so I want to clear this up: Do NOT make the vanilla pudding according to the package directions. I know it seems strange, but go ahead and add the dry instant pudding mix right in with the other ingredients. It really works… I promise!

State Fair Cream Puffs

Makes 1 dozen

1 cup water

1/4 cup (1/2 stick) butter, softened

1/4 teaspoon salt

1 cup all-purpose flour

4 eggs, at room temperature

1 egg yolk

2 tablespoons milk

2 cups (1 pint) heavy cream

1/3 cup confectioners' sugar, plus extra for sprinkling

2 teaspoons vanilla extract

1 Preheat oven to 400°F. In a medium saucepan, bring water, butter, and salt to a boil over medium-high heat. Add flour all at once and stir quickly until mixture forms a ball; remove from heat.

2 Add 1 egg and beat hard with a wooden spoon to blend. Add remaining whole eggs one at a time, beating well after each addition; each egg must be completely blended in before the next egg is added. As you beat it, it will change from an almost-curdled to a smooth appearance. When smooth, spoon 12 mounds of dough onto a large baking sheet.

4 In a small bowl, combine the egg yolk and milk; mix well and brush over dough. Bake 25 to 30 minutes, until golden. Remove to a wire rack to cool completely.

5 In a large bowl, beat cream with an electric beater until soft peaks form. Add confectioners' sugar and vanilla and beat until stiff peaks form. Split cream puffs, fill with cream mixture, and replace tops. Serve immediately or keep chilled. Sprinkle with confectioners' sugar before serving.

TV Tidbit: This recipe comes from the Wisconsin State Fair, where I taped a bunch of shows. I recall there was a lot of tasting during that shoot!

Raspberry Bread Pudding

Serves 6 to 8

4 eggs

1-3/4 cups milk

1/2 cup sugar

1/8 teaspoon salt

1 (12-ounce) bag frozen fresh raspberries (not in syrup)

4 thick slices Hawaiian sweet bread, cut into 1-inch cubes (about 7 cups)

1 Preheat oven to 325°F. Coat a 2-quart baking dish with nonstick cooking spray.

2 In a large bowl, combine eggs, milk, sugar, and salt; mix well. Add raspberries and bread cubes and toss gently to mix well. Pour into baking dish.

3 Bake 45 minutes, or until knife inserted in center comes out clean. Serve warm or chill until ready to use.

SERVING TIP: This one does double-duty as a brunch dish or dessert, so take your pick and serve it as is or topped with whipped cream, ice cream, a sprinkle of confectioners' sugar, or with this amazing homemade sauce.

Vanilla Sauce

Makes about 4 cups

3-1/2 cups cold milk

1 (4-serving-size) package vanilla instant pudding and pie filling

1 teaspoon vanilla extract

3 tablespoons brandy or liqueur, any flavor (optional) (see Note)

1 In a large bowl, combine milk, pudding mix, and vanilla; whisk until well blended. Add brandy, if desired, and continue whisking until thoroughly blended.

2 Chill at least one hour, or until slightly thickened, before using.

NOTE: If you include brandy or liqueur, then keep this as an adults-only sauce.

Crème Brûlée

Serves 4

2 cups (1 pint) heavy cream

1/2 cup milk

1 cup sugar, divided

6 egg yolks

1 tablespoon Amarulla, almond or hazelnut liqueur, optional

1 In a large saucepan, combine heavy cream, milk, 1/2 cup sugar, the egg yolks, and liqueur, if desired, over medium heat and cook 30 minutes, stirring frequently; be careful not to boil.

2 Remove from heat and beat 5 to 6 minutes, or until smooth and thick. Pour equally into 4 (1-cup) custard cups. Chill 4 to 6 hours, or until custard is very firm.

SERVING TIP: These can be topped with melted sugar and chilled for up to 2 hours before serving so, if making these in advance, plan to top with the sugar within 2 hours of serving.

3 In a medium skillet, melt remaining 1/2 cup sugar over medium heat until golden then pour over chilled custards; chill 15 to 20 minutes, or until sugar hardens. Serve, or keep chilled until ready to serve (see Tip).

TV Tidbit: This recipe comes from a colleague of mine who brought it back from Africa (along with the African liqueur Amarulla). I included it in one of my week-long travel specials, and it drew lots of requests!

Our Own Donuts

Makes 10 donuts

Vegetable oil

1 (7.5-ounce) package refrigerated country-style biscuits (10 biscuits)

1/4 cup confectioners' sugar

SERVING TIP: Enjoy these as is, or sprinkled with cinnamon, drizzled with melted chocolate or a sugar glaze, or coated with frosting and some rainbow sprinkles.

1 In a soup pot, heat 1 inch of oil over medium-high heat until hot but not smoking.

2 Separate biscuits and lay flat on a cutting board. Using an apple corer or a plastic soda bottle cap, cut out a small circle in the center of each biscuit, forming rings.

3 Place rings and "holes" in the hot oil a few at a time and cook 1 to 2 minutes, or until golden, turning halfway through cooking.

4 Drain donuts on a paper towel-lined platter. Sprinkle with confectioners' sugar and serve immediately.

Black and White Cookies

Makes 18 cookies

1 (18-1/4-ounce) package white cake mix (see Option)

2/3 cup vegetable oil

2 eggs

8 ounces (half a 16-ounce container) chocolate frosting

8 ounces (half a 16-ounce container) vanilla frosting

1 Preheat oven to 350°F. Coat two cookie sheets with nonstick cooking spray.

2 In a large bowl, combine cake mix, oil, and eggs; mix well. Drop by heaping tablespoonfuls 2 inches apart onto cookie sheets. Bake 12 to 14 minutes, or until firm.

3 Remove cookies to wire racks to cool completely. Frost half of the flat side of each cookie with vanilla frosting and the other half with chocolate frosting. Serve, or cover loosely until ready to serve.

VIEWER FEEDBACK: I got lots of emails about this recipe 'cause everybody said it brought back childhood memories of their favorite bakery classic!

Triple Chocolate Chip Cookies

Makes 3 to 4 dozen

2 cups all-purpose flour

1 teaspoon baking soda

1/2 teaspoon salt

1/2 cup (1 stick) butter, softened

1/2 cup vegetable shortening

3/4 cup granulated sugar

3/4 cup packed light brown sugar

1 teaspoon vanilla extract

1 egg

1 cup (6 ounces) semisweet chocolate chips

1 cup (6 ounces) milk chocolate chips

1 cup (6 ounces) white chocolate chips

1/2 cup chopped walnuts, optional

1 Preheat oven to 375°F.

2 In a medium bowl, combine flour, baking soda, and salt; set aside.

3 In a large bowl, combine butter, shortening, granulated and brown sugars, and vanilla; beat until creamy. Beat in the egg then gradually add flour mixture until well combined. With a wooden spoon, stir in chocolate chips and nuts; mix well.

4 Drop mixture by rounded teaspoonfuls 2 inches apart onto ungreased cookie sheets.

5 Bake 8 to 10 minutes, until golden. Cool 2 minutes then remove cookies to a wire rack to cool completely.

DID YOU KNOW...there's an easy way to soften brown sugar that has hardened? Place it in a microwave-safe container, add a slice of bread, cover, and pop it in the microwave for 15 seconds. The moisture from the bread will create steam that'll soften the sugar. That's it...easy!

Sunny Lemon Squares

Makes 12 to 15 squares

2-1/2 cups all-purpose flour, divided

1 cup (2 sticks) butter or margarine, softened

1 cup confectioners' sugar, plus extra for topping

2 cups granulated sugar

4 eggs

1/2 cup lemon juice

1 teaspoon lemon extract

1 Preheat oven to 350°F. In a medium bowl, combine 2 cups flour, the butter, and confectioners' sugar; mix until crumbly. Press into the bottom of a 9" x 13" baking dish to form a crust; bake 15 minutes.

2 Meanwhile, in a large bowl, with an electric beater on medium speed, beat the remaining 1/2 cup flour, granulated sugar, eggs, lemon juice, and lemon extract until well blended. Pour over hot crust. Bake 25 to 30 minutes, or until set.

3 Allow to cool then cut into squares. Dust with extra confectioners' sugar and serve.

TV Tidbit: This recipe was chosen for my show especially to encourage parents and kids to get into the kitchen together. It makes learning fun when you can teach your little ones math, language, reading, measuring and other skills while cooking and baking. And you get the bonus of sharing goodies when you're done!

Ice Cream Brownie Bowl

Serves 10 to 12

1 (19- to 21-ounce) package brownie mix

1/3 cup Heath® bits

About 1 quart vanilla ice cream, softened

About 2 cups whipped cream *or* whipped topping

1 Preheat oven and prepare brownie mix according to package directions, folding Heath bits into the batter. Bake in a 9″ x 13″ baking pan according to package directions. Under-bake brownies slightly (for a chewier consistency) and let cool thoroughly.

2 Meanwhile, line a round (2-1/2-quart) bowl with plastic wrap. Place about 2/3 of the brownies into the bowl in big chunks; press brownies together, molding them into the bowl, up to about an inch from the top of the bowl.

3 Spoon vanilla ice cream into the bowl, and press it firmly over brownie crust, completely covering it. Place remaining brownies over top and press firmly into ice cream. Cover with plastic wrap and freeze overnight.

SERVING TIP: Remove top layer of plastic wrap, invert bowl onto a serving platter and thaw about 10 minutes. Wrap bowl with a warm dishtowel and let stand for a few minutes. Remove bowl then remaining plastic wrap. Cover top with whipped cream (and maybe even some chocolate or rainbow sprinkles).

Frozen Peanut Butter Squares

Serves 12 to 15

3 cups finely crushed cream-filled chocolate sandwich cookies (about 30 cookies) (see Tip)

6 tablespoons butter, melted

2-1/2 cups heavy cream

1 (14-ounce) can sweetened condensed milk

1 cup peanut butter

1 (3.29-ounce) king-sized Snickers® candy bar, coarsely chopped

1 In a medium bowl, combine cookie crumbs and butter; mix well. Press into bottom of a 9" x 13" baking dish; set aside.

2 In a large bowl, using an electric mixer, beat heavy cream until stiff peaks form. Add sweetened condensed milk and peanut butter, and beat until thoroughly mixed.

3 Spoon peanut butter mixture evenly into cookie crust. Sprinkle chopped candy on top, cover, and freeze 4 hours, or overnight.

TIMESAVING TIP: A quick trick for the cookies is to place them in a resealable plastic storage bag and use a can or other hard object to finely crush them. It's easy and there's no mess! *Check out how amazing this looks on the book cover!*

Index